GOOD GRIEF

FINDING LIGHT IN THE EMOTIONAL DEPTHS OF LIFE

CARDINAL
PUBLISHING HOUSE

To every healing heart, may you find the goodness in grief.

CONTENTS

FOREWORD BY
A MONIQUE ALVAREZ

Grief.

A word that sends chills down our spine. Many experts, philosophers, and teachers have attempted to understand it. Perhaps learning about it can be helpful. I did not find this to be true for myself. Stages of grief, a timeline, a path through it, these are theories at best.

I was introduced to grief five years ago when I gave birth to baby that never took a breath earth side.

I said many times that it was the greatest force I had ever went up against, but I found that also to be untrue. Grief was not my greatest enemy, but it did turn me against myself and that was the battle I could not win.

Grief is unpredictable and cruel. It can grab us by the ankles and drag us to the pit of hell in a flash. Some will tell you grief never goes away. Some say it takes different forms and you just learn how to deal with it. I had bought into this, but I also had a deep desire to challenge it.

I was sitting in a room with three thousand people in Denver,

Colorado listening to Joe Dispenza speak. He started on this topic of grief and I could feel it was about to unravel for me.

Grief, pain, and suffering live in the mind, through our memories. If I had no memory of what had happened, would I be suffering? No. And if we could pull the mind out of the body, would I feel the physical affects of grief? No.

Right there I saw every element of my suffering as optional.

Winter didn't have to throw me backwards. Mother's Day didn't have to be a month of tears. I didn't have to see a baby girl and question every decision I made during my pregnancy. I didn't have to keep track of every date and anniversary. I did not have to attack myself or make myself wrong for any of it.

I had chosen how I grieved. I allowed myself to be angry. I let pure rage course through my mind and body on the regular. I was mad at God, my daughter, and myself. I was mad that I had to keep going. I was mad that my kids lost me when I lost her. I was angry my husband was left with a shell of a woman. And now I felt the opportunity to be done with grief. I wasn't going to deny it's presence, I was outgrowing my need for it.

I was sick of telling the story. I was tired of saying I lost a baby. It didn't feel true. I actually didn't lose anything and in the most bizarre of ways I was gifted the opportunity to grow into someone I had no idea I could be.

Grief is not a life sentence, but it a masterful teacher that we can sit with as long as we want to.

One man's words brought me to a new place and that is what is in your hands, the stories of those who have walked with grief and their words have the power to bring you to a new place, the one you have been longing for.

There is no right or wrong on this journey. It's yours and yours alone. There is no timeline or linear path. There's plenty of ups and downs, twists and turns. For this moment, I am here to remind you of who you really are, beyond loss, death, and grief.

Place your hands on your heart.

You are a solid oak tree.

Your roots run deep and your branches reach the sky.

You are life, you are breath, you are light.

You hold love.

You are a blessing to many.

You are the answer to many prayers.

You are the gift.

You have what it takes.

You are surrounded and supported.

You are never alone.

You have the wisdom and experience.

You can smile at your future.

You are strength.

You are a warrior.

You are not done.

Everything you need for today and for tomorrow are with you.

You always have what you need, when you need it.

Thank you for continuing, especially on the days you didn't think you could.

Keep looking for the silver lining and keep mining for the gold.

Keep the fire burning in your bones.

Keep your head held high.

Nothing is bigger than you, not even grief.

INTRODUCTION

When the title "Good Grief" found me, I was scared. Much like society does with grief, I tried to ignore it and push it away. *Grief, a good thing?* Most people don't think so. Most people don't give grief the opportunity to gift them. When we have the courage and resources to acknowledge and actually feel our grief, we open the door to healing, spaciousness, and freedom. In redefining our relationship with grief, we discover new layers of the human experience. Grief gets to be part of our journey, but it doesn't have to define it.

Wherever you are on your healing journey, may you remember you're not alone. May these stories remind you that feeling is healing, that your softness is one of your strengths, and that healing happens in community.

This collection of stories about grief, loss, hope, and renewal offers a necessary conversation about one of the very things that makes us human: love.

CHAPTER ONE

THE ART OF GRIEVING

ANTJE HOWARD

I am sharing a part of my grieving journey, which for me also turned into a creative journey. Even though it will always hurt to live with my loss, I began a search for beauty and new meaning in my story. Also, I want to make space to express and experience grief honestly and openly. I found great depth and creative power in my own experience, and I hope that you will also see the healing potential of art in the grieving process. My intention is to share my healing story, and at the same time, I hope that it will inspire you to search for your own creative expression. This is how my art helped me, and I believe this healing is accessible to you as well.

I dedicate this chapter to my son Lukas Vincent Howard, who is the reason and inspiration for this work.

WHEN THERE ARE NO WORDS, THERE IS STILL ART

My personal grief journey began very abruptly and in a quite traumatic way. I was thirty weeks pregnant with a little boy, anxious about the future, and full of plans, expectations, and dreams. And then one day, my baby stopped moving, and from one moment to the next everything changed. My husband Jay took me to the hospital, and we found out that our baby had unexpectedly died. There was no explanation, nothing we could do, just this unbelievable message ringing in our ears, and the feeling that our life was suddenly falling apart. I had to endure the long and slow process of induced labor. And after days of crying and asking the same questions over and over without any answer, I started drawing right there in the hospital.

I could not think, could not speak, could not understand what was happening, or express myself and my feelings in any way. So I started drawing lines in my sketchbook and looked at the chaos I felt inside me. I began to recognize myself in there, trapped in the web of emotions, thoughts, and pain. While my body was going through contractions, I went deeper into the drawing, not to get away from reality, but rather in an attempt to see what was unfolding inside me. After a while, I noticed a big circle emerge on the edge of my page, and I realized that there had to be something beyond this never-ending painful moment. I extended my picture onto the next page to give space and form to that big circle. I knew that there had to be a way to move forward and beyond this moment. So, I started to draw my way there, even though I had no idea how I would ever get there. It helped my mind to move, and change, slowly but surely, and I began to imagine that this was not the end of our story. I had that picture with me when I finally birthed my son. It reminded me, and gave me strength, because I had seen and believed that there was something beyond. I held on to invisible threads that pulled me through the hardest parts of this experience. They pulled me toward a future that was yet unwritten, but I knew it was there, waiting.

The next day, I added some very meaningful words onto the pages that Jay had said: "Our strength will last longer than our pain". We made a promise to each other that day, that this experience would not break us, but make us stronger. We had no idea how, or what it would look like, but I kept holding on to this intention over the coming difficult weeks and months. And I kept making art, kept expressing myself without words. And with my art, I slowly found new words and new meaning. I saw that I was still here, life was still happening, and I was still a part of it.

ART AS A HEALING PRACTICE

The Neurographica® drawing method that I practice and work with helped me through the most challenging experience of my life so far. I will be forever grateful that I had this tool in my hands, not because it made the process any easier, or allowed me to run away into a fantasy world, but because it allowed me to consciously be with what is. In a way, it enabled me to adjust my mind to the reality that I could not change or run away from.

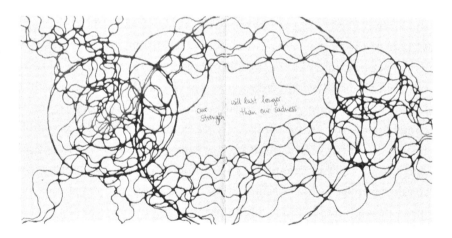

I first learned about Neurographica® a few years back as a mindful drawing practice and self-coaching method. I remember how I was immediately captivated by its beauty, by its simplicity, and aesthetic appeal. But there was much more than that. In 2020 I took a yearlong training to become a Neurographica® instructor and learned to appreciate this method as a tool for deep self-exploration and reflection. Neurographica® uses simple visual elements, like circles and lines, and connects all elements in a drawing into a whole, into a visual web of our reality. In the process we can give meaning to individual elements, naming the things we see. On the paper, we visually adjust what we want to change in reality. This does not mean that the things we draw will just magically appear, but it helps the mind to perceive that there is always a possibility for change. Neurographica® was created by a Russian-Israeli psychology professor and artist named Pavel Piskarev with exactly this idea in mind, that when we can change our minds, our perception and interpretation of life's events, we will also be able to change our reality.

Neurographica® provides a structure, a safe and clear space, and a linear step-by-step process. This ordered process enables us to let go, dive deep into the subconscious, and allow new and unexpected ideas to form. Each drawing begins with a theme, an intention, or a question that we then express in a visually abstract way. Throughout the drawing process, we observe all parts of the self, the subtle signals of the body, the emotions that are arising, and the thoughts as they appear and change. In this meditative process, all the parts of our being are involved in creating an answer, and a new inner reality. It is a holistic approach to creativity, and I have witnessed many times how it can bring completely unexpected and truly incredible results. We focus on the process, the little changes in our perception, and the journey of creation as it unfolds through our hands. The resulting image is like an imprint of that process, a blueprint of our inner development. And it can help remind us to keep moving in that new direction.

I experience this type of drawing as a great healing tool—a tool that now accompanies me on my grief journey. It allows me to witness myself and my grieving process through my art. Over time, I can see how my themes and questions are slowly changing, and with them, my experience of the moment is changing as well. Neurographica® allows me to deeply understand and embody this change. It helps me return to the ever-changing flow of life as a creator, and not remain stuck as a victim of my misfortune.

LEARNING TO BE WITH CHANGE

When I begin a drawing, I always start with what is now. I find a visual expression of the moment and then mindfully create changes from there. In grief, it can be very hard to be with what is now. We can encounter unbelievable pain, disappointment, and loneliness, and there are countless reasons to hide from this "what is". However, I found it very helpful to come back to the reality of the moment, to consciously reflect on where I am, to witness my good days and my bad days. The process allows me to practice acceptance, which is very crucial in my own healing. When I acknowledge all the feelings and thoughts that are present, I can go on from there. The journey out of pain needs an honest starting point.

I know how in the midst of grief you can completely forget your own well-being. But when you know and accept what you feel, it is much easier to express it, to ask for help, to set boundaries, and to make the time and space that you need for your own healing. You can learn to see your own needs from a different perspective, with deeper compassion, and ask for support from an inner realization and understanding of your own needs. Drawing in an honest and reflective way is true self-care. You can always ask the picture what you need right now. You can call in support, drawing it on paper and then allowing your mind to create it.

Dealing with my grief taught me to take care of myself in a completely new way. But grief does not always feel the same. I realized very quickly in my own process how unpredictable my feelings could be. My emotional, mental, and physical state changed a lot, all the time. It can be messy and overwhelming, but in the end, it always changes. So I allowed my grief to change over and over. For several months, I kept drawing my pain, my guilt, my shame, my sadness, and then finally my anger. I found out a lot about myself in these quite challenging processes. The drawing was not always fun, but it always revealed something new, whenever I was ready to see it. Everything becomes softer as it is seen, recognized, and embraced.

During the drawing, I create a visible flow in the picture. This also creates an inner flow, an openness for change, and I can begin to move and release what has been stuck.

Grief and loss can literally erase all colors from the world. Everything is tainted in gray. Have you ever asked yourself what color your grief is, or what your anger looks like today?

In the drawing, we can explore even deeper layers of these emotions, with the help of color. Even though it might feel inaccessible at first to create something colorful, it will have a healing effect once you let color come back into your life.

For me, a shift happened when I included my son Lukas as a little circle in one of my drawings. I asked myself what color he had and felt a light orange. It was such an uplifting feeling, and I experienced a deep connection to him in that moment. I knew it was time to bring color back into my life, as a healing energy that I could consciously awaken and surround myself with. The process of applying color can be very meditative and soothing in itself. I usually introduce color very slowly and in layers, using colored pencils. I like this way of drawing because it gives me time to feel into it, to recognize which color makes me feel better, or how it influences my inner state at that moment. The effects are present while I am drawing, and there is a visual footprint of the process that I can come back to later. Color adds a new dimension of meaning to all elements in the drawing. I believe that color has healing effects on many different levels, and you can actively bring those into your life with the help of art.

I still come back to experience certain emotions again and again, and sometimes it feels like falling back or going in circles. But when I accept, make space, and observe my emotions and thoughts very closely, I see that I am slowly changing all the time. Giving myself time to reflect in a creative way has brought back my trust in the process and a new appreciation for each moment.

CONSCIOUSLY CREATING A NEW SELF

Every big life change brings the struggle of finding a new identity. For me, it was crucial to create new meaning in my daily experience and my loss. This is a very personal journey and it will look different for everyone, so I will only share what I found as part of my story. At first, my identity was simply shattered. I felt like there was a huge hole inside me, and there was nothing that could ever fill or repair it. I was facing the task of creating a new Self that could incorporate the past, the present, and a yet unknown future. Art can be a powerful tool for integrating and reshaping contradictory experiences into a consistent whole. We rediscover ourselves in the moment, here and now, and at the same time honor, purify, and transform our memories and emotions.

I felt a profound change when I began to think of my son not only as the baby I lost and will miss forever, but I discovered him as my teacher—the greatest teacher I could ever imagine. I wanted to honor Lukas as my teacher in a drawing process that I created for my Art of Grieving group. For this drawing, we wrote a letter to our loved ones and included elements of it into the drawing, intuitively picking a sentence or words from the letter. After a significant loss there might be many things that remain unsaid, questions that will never be answered. We can communicate these in writing, and acknowledge whatever comes up in the process. When we become conscious of our thoughts and work with them as part of the creative process, we can again gain a new and deeper understanding. My own words tell a new story. They become part of the web of meaning that I weave through my art. I create new meaning with every picture and can slowly integrate my experiences, coming back to them in a gentle and loving way.

Drawing immediately became my guide and witness on my grieving journey. I believe that all humans are meant to create, and I know how much creativity is hidden in difficult life experiences like loss. My drawings bring healing on various levels. I recognize the effects in my everyday life, in my relationships, and in my communication with the world. I am more aware of, and able to be with what comes up in the moment. I feel deeper and develop greater compassion and patience with myself and others. Drawing and deeply reflecting helps me live from a place of inner empowerment. My new Self slowly forms as an ever-changing and precious gift that includes all of me. I honor my memories, past experiences, and challenges, I acknowledge my path, my power, and my choices, and I celebrate my achievements. The story of my loss has many teachings. It gives me access to deep inner experiences as well as a new perspective on life itself, and I am grateful for that.

GETTING BACK IN TOUCH WITH THE WORLD

About five months into my grief journey, I felt called to share some of my processes and create a supportive group space that included drawing. When I openly spoke about our baby's death and shared some precious drawings on social media, I received personal messages from so many people, many of whom I had never met. Whenever I opened the space to freely share, by telling my own story, people were there. It was a bitter-sweet feeling to know that I was not at all alone in my fate. Just usually people would not talk about it. I felt a deep inner motivation to make space and share the healing power I experienced through my art. In June 2022, I began the Art of Grieving Journey as a supportive and creative group space for people who are grieving.

Guiding a group is part of my own healing process and my search for meaning and purpose. It allows me to create something that supports others. Here, Neurographica® helps me guide others through visual experiences and into deep inner processes. I lead the drawing process into a meditative inquiry. The method gives me a structure and a visual alphabet to depict and visually explore experiences, emotions, and other related themes. It helps me draw a road map for others, where they can create and witness their own story.

It is especially healing for me to talk about the process and witness the great variety of experiences and stories that my group shares. It helps tremendously to listen to the perspectives of others who are on this path of healing. I learned again how many different faces the emotion we call grief really has. It is part of our human story and yet shows up in a different way for everyone. It is unpredictable, surprising, and irritating, and we often search for a way to control it. But it can also be our greatest teacher.

We focus on different aspects of grief in each drawing. This makes this very big theme more accessible, and we can discover the many layers of it. With the Art of Grieving, I offer myself and others the opportunity to bring the different faces of grief to the surface and move through them with the support of the group. We can use these creative processes to find ways to continue on with our lives and at the same time honor the need to grieve, remember, and acknowledge all that is. With these art processes, we feel the continuity of life after loss, and experience our own creative role in it. I offer this support group monthly, on a donation basis, and the first drawing process in the series is freely shared on YouTube (link: https://youtu.be/UiWUEgFINv4).

To close this chapter, I invite you to explore this method for yourself. Allow yourself to honor your grief and open a new chapter on your healing journey. My hope is that this will help you to access your creative inner guidance and to find inner peace and meaning in your own grief and healing journey.

ABOUT THE AUTHOR

Antje Howard is an artist, guide, and teacher whose goal is to support self-discovery in a creative way. In 2019, she started exploring NeuroGraphica®, a drawing method that she discovered on her own creative healing journey. This method helped her release self-doubt and perfectionism and developed into a personal practice for deep self-reflection and healing. Antje has an academic background in Education and has creatively supported children, teens, college students, and adults. She is a certified NeuroGraphica® instructor, a QiGong and Meditation teacher, and a dancer. Antje also facilitates Women Circles, and leads movement and dance workshops.

At the beginning of 2022, Antje suffered the loss of her son Lukas at thirty-one weeks pregnant. This experience deeply impacted the trajectory of her creative work and teaching. Antje created the Art of Grieving support group to share the healing power of art and to bring people together through grief and personal growth.

Website: www.neuroartproject.net
Instagram: www.instagram.com/neuroartproject
Youtube: www.youtube.com/user/tarantjel

CHAPTER TWO

THE GIRL BEHIND THE GLASSES

BLÁTHNAID CARLIN

I got my first pair of glasses at the age of two. They were the first thing I put on every morning and the last thing I took off at night.

Throughout my childhood, I hated wearing glasses. Wearing glasses and being perceived as a geek seemed synonymous. Mind you, geek I was and geek I am.

As time went on, I grew to love my glasses. They became and remain a huge part of my identity. They frame my face. I match them with my outfits. They are a part of me.

I remember an incident in junior high school when a girl in my class shouted at me across the classroom: "Bláthnaid! You are the biggest geek." I was humiliated.

But I remember this as a turning point because this was the first time in my life I was happy to have my glasses. I felt safe behind them. I did not want to let the class bully see me cry. I kept my head down for the remainder of the class, and I remember huge droplets of tears landing inside my glasses.

Ironically that moment of prepubescent classroom humiliation forced me to look at myself and truly see my own potential. From that moment on, I had a crystal clear, twenty-twenty vision about where I wanted to go and what I wanted to achieve.

As the years went by, I worked my way through list after list of ambitions, dreams, visions and goals. In the words of Teddy Roosevelt, "Believe you can and you're halfway there."

I truly believed that if I worked hard enough, there wasn't anything I couldn't do.

Throughout my life, a lot of people have assumed I have just been fortunate with the things I have achieved—don't get me wrong, I have been very lucky, and I am so thankful for the opportunities I have had. However, there is not one thing that has just fallen into my lap. Every opportunity I created, I worked and researched, and I had the foresight and the courage to say "yes"!

As women, we are expected to work hard, smile, and not make a song or dance about anything. We are expected to be meek and humble. Instead of being perceived as hard-working and ambitious, we're seen as cold and callous. Instead of confident and proud, we're seen as boastful and big-headed. Instead of passionate and driven, we're seen as emotional and narrow-minded. But hear me now! I make no apologies in saying I am so very proud of myself and everything I have achieved in my life so far.

By age twenty-two, I had one year left of medical school and had met the man of my dreams—everything was right on track. Six years later, we were married. After that, our sights were set on having a family. That was our dream and our vision. Lo and behold, we fell pregnant a month after we were married. We were so delighted. We immediately started to plan and envisage our lives as parents, something we had both yearned for our whole lives.

I cannot begin to describe the devastation when I started to bleed, and when we were told the baby was gone... even now, years later, I cannot put into words the ache I felt in my heart. Our vision hadn't changed; we still yearned to be parents. This has been a valuable life lesson. This experience had to happen for me to fully understand what a broken heart felt like and what not to say to those in pain. That a simple "I'm sorry, what do you need, I'm here for you," or sometimes saying nothing is what a person might need.

We couldn't believe it when we got pregnant again almost immediately. Our rainbow baby!

The devastation when I started to bleed again. This cannot be. I wouldn't believe it. This time felt different. I had a piercing, gut-wrenching, breath-taking pain in my side. I wasn't miscarrying; this was an ectopic pregnancy, in my fallopian tube, and it had ruptured. I knew exactly what was happening when the pain struck.

I needed emergency surgery. The last thing I did before being wheeled into the operating theatre was hand my glasses to my husband. "Keep those safe," I said, "because I'll need them when I wake up."

As soon as the door to the operating room closed, I started to cry. I knew there was a chance I might not wake up, and my glasses would forever be a symbol of grief and loss, the last thing I gave my husband.

Spoiler alert: I didn't die. But the months that followed were overwhelmingly difficult. I was so focused on having a baby, blinkers on, tunnel vision... I felt desperate. I had never known heartache like this before, and I felt cripplingly helpless, useless and powerless. There was nothing I could do and nothing I could control. There is no amount of hard work, vision or determination that can get you pregnant.

Each passing month became an endless cycle of ovulation, trying to conceive—am I pregnant, am I not? Then devastation at the arrival of my period. MONTHS of heartache. I struggled with this overwhelming sense of guilt. I couldn't sleep, and I felt like a failure in all aspects of my life. I felt I could do nothing right.

Fourteen months, almost to the day after my emergency surgery I was back in hospital but this time I was giving birth to our son. All our dreams come true!

Maternity leave was both amazing and exhausting and busy and lonely. I loved being off and getting to know my son and watching him grow and learn and discover. But being a first-time mum was overwhelming. Any time I felt frustrated or drained, I felt so guilty. What was wrong with me? We had yearned for this for so long.

Let me take a moment now to say that hindsight is a wonderful thing. Being a parent is hard. No matter how many books you read on parenting, no matter how prepared you think you are...nothing can prepare you for the tiredness, worry, guilt, happiness, frustration and overwhelming love you have for this tiny little defenceless human you have created. Parents, acknowledge these feelings, allow yourself to feel them, forgive yourself and be kind to yourself. We spend most of our lives inside our own heads, so make it a nice place to be.

We started to try for a little sibling for our son almost immediately after he was born, which added to the already emotional, wonderful, amazing, and exhausting transition. It took us almost a year before we became pregnant with baby number four, our daughter. We were now a family of four with two perfect little humans and our hearts full of love.

I was off on maternity leave again, and it was so lovely watching our children grow together and their wee relationship form and strengthen.

But as the months went on, I began to feel anxious and worried all the time. I wasn't confident going out of the house on my own with the two kids. I tried to convince myself that I was still adjusting to life as a mum of two. I started to believe that perhaps, I was just a bad mum. I had gone from being so driven, ambitious and confident to feeling useless and worthless. Who was I?

Before I knew it, I was back to work, and I discovered I was pregnant again. My fifth pregnancy in as many years. We were thrilled and so thankful to be adding another wee sibling to the brood.

One night, I wakened with an awful cramping pain in my stomach. I went to the bathroom, and when I saw the blood, my heart sank. Another miscarriage.

I was so angry. AGAIN! Are you KIDDING ME!!!

Over the next few weeks, I faded; my heart was shattered; I felt obsolete; I had failed again.

As the days and weeks passed, the light that once danced in the eyes behind my glasses faded and faded, and it felt like it went out completely. I lost ALL my confidence. I couldn't make even the simplest of decisions. I did not want to be alone with our two amazing, perfect, wonderful children. I was convinced I was going to say something or do something that would emotionally scar them or damage them for the rest of their wee lives. I was having awful daily chest pain. I didn't even have the energy to load clothes into the washing machine or wash the dishes. I would go straight to bed when my husband came home from work. I felt utterly useless. I honestly thought I would never feel happy again. I had lost myself; I had no insight, and everything seemed dark.

It took me months of tears, counselling, support from my family doctor, self-reflection, self-care, and challenging my inner thoughts of guilt and negativity. Slowly but surely, the fog started to lift. I began to see things more clearly, my confidence grew, the good days began to outnumber the bad days, and I started enjoying life again. My insight returned and that insight gradually turned into vision.

After five months off, I returned to work, and for the first time in years, I felt like the old me. My inner geek is back, and she is powerful and full of energy and ideas.

I am dreaming, creating vision boards, compiling bucket lists and planning for the future.

Three years on... I am stronger and more confident than ever. I have learned and accepted that adversity is an inevitability in life, but I know now it is how we deal with and overcome that adversity that truly defines us. That is resilience.

Maya Angelou famously said, "People will forget what you said and people with forget what you did, but people will never forget how you made them feel." How true are those words? I keep that in mind each and every day. I try to spread love and positivity wherever and whenever I can. Whether that's in my work with my patients, in my personal life with family and friends or in the randomness of everyday encounters with strangers in the sharing of a smile or a random act of kindness. It is in doing those things that I keep my heart full, my spirits high and my confidence where it should be. We truly rise by lifting others.

Truth be told, I still have my bad days, like everyone. I still struggle with imposter syndrome and perfectionism issues. I know I have unattainably high standards for myself. I have worked too hard to build myself up and put myself back together again, and I continue to do so each and every day for the rest of my life. I will not let my confidence waiver again.

To anyone out there struggling, no matter how lost you feel, no matter how dark it seems, there is always hope.

There is always light.

Just put one foot in front of the other.

Take it one hour; one minute; one second at a time.

Celebrate all your wins even if your win for that day is mustering up the energy to brush your teeth or get out of bed.

I am extremely proud of myself and everything I have overcome.

My scars both emotional and physical are my war paint, and much like my glasses, I wear them with pride.

ABOUT THE AUTHOR

Bláthnaid Carlin is a 36-year-old medical doctor from Ireland. She is a wife and mother of two who describes herself as a family woman to the core. Bláthnaid has spoken very openly about her struggles with pregnancy loss, miscarriage, and ectopic pregnancy and strives to break the taboo surrounding all women's issues. Bláthnaid is also a classically trained violinist and singer and is no stranger to the stage. She toured as an Irish dancer with the National Dance Company of Ireland. Bláthnaid was also nominated for and won Inspirational Doctor of the Year 2022. Bláthnaid is passionate about celebrating diversity and promoting equality. She is an LGBTQI ally and is fervent in the fight against climate change. As a doctor, Bláthnaid deals with grief each and every day. She loves her job and is humbled and privileged to be able to help patients through the best and worst times of their lives. She hoped that sharing her personal experience with grief might lessen the burden of others beyond her consultation room.

Instagram: @blathnaidcarlin
Twitter: @carlin_dr

CHAPTER THREE

KANGA

CLÉA HERNANDEZ

CANIS EX MACHINA

"**W**hen will you write the book about her?**"**
Every so often my father asks me this question. I don't remember the first time he asked. I do know that in my family, we were all struck with love at odd angles within the first few weeks of her life.

For me, the first strike was keenly targeted and almost at first sight.

Tanit, our family dog, gave birth to a litter of Andalusian Hound puppies at our home in Maryland. They were born on Thursday, May 13, 2004, and I was twenty-five years old and living with roommates in a row house in DC at the time. I finished my work week and came home to meet them on Saturday.

Tanit was nursing her seven pups in the whelping box when I arrived. I climbed in to lie down with them and one of them self-propelled onto my neck to nuzzle me. It took impressive agility for a still-blind newborn with limited motor control. Like her siblings and parents she was a golden cinnamon color with white markings, except blonder, and with half a white streak up the left side of her neck, like a collar she'd broken clean through.

I asked what her name was. My stepdad said they called her Kanga.

This is just a chapter of her book; someday I'll have healed enough to write her whole story.

THE TRICKSTER

Most dog owners think their dog is the smartest to ever live, and I'm not going to try to convince you that mine was smarter than yours or anyone else's. How do you quantify canine intelligence? If we bothered to argue over it, you could point out that she was the most remedial student in obedience training. Then I'd say that if you didn't know her and weren't paying attention, you might not see her plan. She learned the tricks before any of the other dogs, but because she was focused on the long con of getting the treats for free instead of the instant gratification of doing the trick for a treat, she held out and graduated at the very bottom of her class. She trained us all to give her the treats anyway. No one understood the irrelevance of a diploma more than she did, and the photo of her on my lap wearing a cap and gown is a family joke.

My mom always told visitors, when they dropped by to meet the puppies, that she marched to the beat of her own drum. It was a nice way of saying she was more of a mob boss from outer space than a dog, and it was often followed by a gentle warning to keep close watch over any snacks. The others did puppy things, like chew furniture, eat rocks, or chase bugs. She observed, calculated, and orchestrated. We had our suspicions that she was framing the others for the major crimes, but she left no clues behind.

After distracting her brothers and sisters from playing with a toy, she would circle back to the toy and examine its weak points and textural anomalies for the most efficient method of evisceration. I couldn't tell you how much money I wasted on "indestructible" dog toys that died disturbingly creative deaths within an hour.

She didn't care much for the dog park, or canine politics, as I imagine she saw it. She was faster than every other dog except the greyhounds, and they were only able to outrun her because of the longer leg technicality. Once she had proven her superior speed, she lost interest in interacting with strange dogs. She always liked cats better; maybe because they shared her aloofness and smelled vaguely of prey.

Kanga possessed a mix of primal hunger, natural athleticism, and intellectual mischief that made her the cutest little apex predator. In her youth, she left a trail of rodent bodies behind in every up-and-coming neighborhood we lived in. She was a master escape artist and could almost always figure out how to slip her halter or collar; when she couldn't, she'd lure me into a false sense of security while walking and then make a break for it when the leash went slack. She came up empty in only two leash-free hunts throughout her long, storied life: once with a squirrel who turned and slashed her nose when she caught it, then made a break for it; and once with a skunk. You can imagine how the skunk escaped.

For all her self-possession, she and I belonged to each other. From that first bonding in the whelping box, she attached herself to me with a magnetic intention that is hard to think of as anything other than preordained love carried through past lives. She was sweet with people, if a bit Machiavellian, though she favored the journey and had no problem saying goodbye to anyone else. It was different for us. I felt physical pain when we had to separate for any reason. Her cries when I left for work were visceral, soul-rending sobs.

When my husband came into our lives later, I joked (but not really) with him that Kanga would always be the love of my life. My dad has always said that she couldn't have found a bigger sucker, and he's right: although I never intended to take home one of those puppies, she had me at that first nuzzle.

THE SWAMP

We were kids together. Kanga performed the trick of teaching me to stay young as the years passed while bestowing the crushing gift of motherhood on me. Any human animal who loves and accepts responsibility for the life of another animal with a shorter lifespan knows the cold shadow that creeps over the sun on even the happiest, most carefree days. But while people are conditioned to be anxious, fractured mental time travelers, haunted by the past and stalked by the future, dogs are mindfulness mentors. They teach us to focus here, now; now is where they always live, and as long as they're with you, it's heaven.

I like to think we were uncommonly wild and brave as a unit, and so really only afraid of one thing: losing each other. Lacking that human fear of death, however, our priorities differed, and her predatory instincts betrayed us on some fateful occasions.

One day, when she was one week shy of a year old, we drove out to a small beach in Virginia with my roommates for a friend's birthday. Eight 20-somethings and two dogs packed into our friend Fernando's Volkwagon bus that he called the Family Wagon—a well-worn vehicle that could have its own biopic.

We parked in a wooded clearing around midday and hauled our supplies to the shoreline while Kanga heaved at her leash, thirty-five pounds of pure muscle. She was interested in a stinky bog just between the ocean and the woods. I imagine the few hours of joy and peace we enjoyed there as the backdrop for a heist-planning montage unfolding in her brain.

After a few drinks, I was in a state of mind to be convinced she wouldn't go far if I let her off the leash. For the first half hour or so, she ran around the group in a neat little orbit—chasing seagulls, stealing toys from small children, standing on her hind legs and pushing the children onto their butts when they stole the toys back and taunted her with them. Everything was *fine*.

No surprise, she made a break for it. Right into the reeds behind us that obscured the swamp beyond from view.

I called for her and she didn't come. I circled the bog looking for movement, listening for rustles. Nothing. I started to cry out for her in panic, and my friends rushed over to join the search party. We walked around parting reeds, only to find more reeds and gross smells. About fifteen minutes later, we heard something: a piercing nasal squeal from deep in the center of the bog. I realized she couldn't open her mouth to vocalize as she normally would have.

Later, when Fernando retold this story, he said it was like watching a war movie when I charged the swamp. I couldn't see her, couldn't tell which direction her cry came from. My sandals were sucked off my feet into the sludge, and I kept charging because nothing else mattered. I pulled myself across the sludge reed by reed, waist deep, tears streaming, throat raw from screaming her name. Horrified that if I could be in this deep, she must be drowning entirely in this shit, and I might never be able to find her.

In the distance a pack of dogs were barking, and a man's voice was yelling at them — or me — to shut up. Then he yelled, "Hey, your dog is out here!" I dragged myself out of the swamp and started running up the hill I heard the dogs barking from, but something stopped me. I turned back to the swamp and scanned it one more time. There, peering from behind a tree, was a very black dog. I called her again and she ran into my arms, shivering and squealing with relief and fright. She was completely covered in bog muck up to her little pink nose.

From that experience, I learned what it really meant to have a life in my hands. I was struck by how close to losing her I had come, and couldn't release the fear that one day we would not get the happy ending.

GOLDEN EARS

We took great care of each other and had more happy, healthy years together than most dogs and their people get—almost seventeen. Kanga was my protector and a fierce warrior queen. After Washington, D.C., we moved to Montreal for four years where we spent the long winters trudging through the snow on Mount Royal and our summers at sidewalk cafes holding court while people told her she was *tres jolie*. But God forbid anyone should act erratically near me! She could shapeshift from Bambi to wolf and back fast enough to give you whiplash.

When we left Montreal to return to the States, it was in a Craigslist rideshare with just one suitcase, headed for New York City. We stopped off in Philly to visit my friend Tom. He and I ended up dating, so Kanga and I stayed in Philly and Tom and I got married three years later. She wasn't a fan at first but grew to love him once he gave up trying to discipline her.

From Philly, we moved to Savannah, Georgia, to escape winter and stayed for the rest of her life. I believe she was happier there in her golden years than she had ever been. I could work from home more and she had a yard of her own to hunt in, well-stocked with Southern critters and their interesting poops.

THE SHADOW

On Valentine's Day of 2019, she had a seizure, and we found out she had brain cancer. Nothing ever prepares you. Nothing makes the pain easier to bear once the clock starts ticking. Covid shut the world down a month later, and I couldn't have cared less. There was nowhere else I would have wanted to be than holding her in our home.

I learned then that vets don't tend to want to give you estimates of how long you have to say goodbye before things get "bad," because they can't win no matter what they tell you. Your best friend, your baby, the love of your life has Y-Z months, weeks, or days left, where Z equals absolute nothing. Still, you become obsessed with this amorphous timetable (hers was 1-3 months according to the literature, 6-9 months unofficially because I begged our veterinary neurologist for a better-tailored guess. She lived a full year longer).

You become obsessed with the signs of deterioration, fast or slow, and you forget about life. Death is Alpha now, and there is no light at the end of the tunnel. But dogs are persistent little Buddhas. I hugged her and cried non-stop for the first few weeks, and she'd look at me like I was nuts; this was how she trained me to laugh at myself, and soon the quantum logic of her love brought me all the way back to her for the time we had left.

In that last year, she taught me what it means to live every moment with intention. The tumor grew and altered her motor functions, and with precision, she adjusted. Although she appeared to be happy and pain-free, she no longer knew where her back half was in space. Her tail became incrementally more crooked over time because she used it to guide her descent when sitting down. When she sat, she always sprawled one leg out in this super cool posture like she felt no pain at all. The first whiff of meat from across the house was always still enough to get her up again.

She relinquished her trademark gracefulness and somehow became more capable of grace and purpose than ever. I have a video of my last long walk with her a week before she died, hopping joyfully on and off curbs and running as fast as she could—which even then was much faster than I could—diagonally.

And she slept, as ever, curled in the nook behind my knees. Except that she would wet the bed at least once a night and wake herself up, look around for the culprit with a huff, then leave Tom and me in a pool of her urine.

I had a nightmare during our last night together. She and I were in a swamp; she kept swimming away from me, and I couldn't catch up to her fast enough. I could feel the presence of something lurking under the water, waiting for her to be just far enough out of my reach to pull her under. I woke up sobbing. I knew there was nothing more I could do to protect her.

In the months prior, Tom and I had many talks about how we would know when it was time. It was always going to be my decision, and he was there to take care of everything else. He tried to come up with a formula for how we could be sure, bless his heart. I always replied that I was certain she would tell me.

A few hours after I woke up from that dream, she looked straight into my eyes and cried out in pain for me to make it stop. It was very deliberate.

THE WOLF MOTHER

We had a vet come to the house to put her to sleep. The vet was a gentle soul who Kanga welcomed into our final moments as though she had always been part of our family. Tom fixed Kanga a heaping plate of raw N.Y. strip and salmon, and there were just a few bites left by the time the injection in her leg reached her heart. She didn't even notice the needle. Tom stroked her face while I sang into her ear and kissed her neck.

When she was a puppy, my mom always used to tell Kanga that nothing bad would ever happen to her. It was the last thing I said to her. She lived and died with an unshakeable faith in my love for her. Later, I found strength in knowing that.

I lost myself for at least a year afterwards. The bone-deep intuition that had guided me all my life felt cut off at the source. I had lost my cub, and with her, my connection to the part of myself driven by instinct and primal wisdom that hunted what mattered. I drowned myself in work, personal drama, and ego.

But even when I wasn't paying attention, she was always there. Patient. Leaving me trails to follow: signs, scents, memories that trigger awakening.

My great achievement was filling her time on earth with all the love, joy, and protection I was capable of, from the moment she first opened her eyes to the last time she closed them. I like to think that now she asks me to do the same for myself.

A few weeks after she died, I dreamt for the first time that she pushed open the bedroom door with her nose and walked in to check on me. I have that dream every so often. And in certain moments of consciousness, I feel her there in the doorway between this world and the next, waiting for me to come home.

ABOUT THE AUTHOR

Cléa Hernandez is a writer and story architect. Born in Silver Spring, Maryland, Cléa makes herself at home anywhere in the world she can find the best stories. She discovers meaning through adventure with her animal soulmates and the occasional human. A messaging and communications strategist who builds story systems for purpose-driven brands, Cléa consults the collective unconscious for narrative inspiration; she draws strategic psychological insights from archetypal journeys (like the tarot and the monomyth) and behavioral economics principles to inform her branding work. She currently lives in New York City and runs her own brand communications studio, Mythograph.

> *LinkedIn:* www.linkedin.com/in/clea-hernandez-018ab023
> *Website:* www.Mythograph.co

CHAPTER FOUR

IT'S OK TO JUST BE

ERIN MCCAHILL

I boarded the plane like every other time, put my luggage in the bin, pulled out my green mini-iPod and headset and got comfortable for the three-and-a-half-hour flight. The same routine I had done a thousand times before and several times in the last seven weeks, but this time it felt different. I fell asleep as soon as I got buckled in as I always do when thirty minutes into the flight, I was awake thinking we must be landing soon. I looked out the window to find the mountain tops that comfort me, but they were nowhere to be found. All I saw was the large blue sky with white fluffy clouds floating by. Staring out the window wondering where we were I started to replay the last two and a half months and all that transpired. I saw excitement, proud moments, and devasting ones. My eyes got watery, then tiny tears started to trickle down, and then the dam broke. I couldn't stop crying; I lost control, trying to keep my composure in the fully packed plane. It just was not happening. I looked out across the horizon searching for a sign from my mom that she was up here close and near to me—how could it be that she is gone and a new journey in life had just begun at the same time. It doesn't make sense and all I can hold onto is that I was able to share my journey and accomplishments with her in her last few weeks here on earth.

Oh, I kept searching for any sign, but there was no sign in sight, only increasing tears that couldn't stop. Mom had just passed away, and the emptiness and silence was real, raw, and uncomfortable. This was a new world once again. I couldn't control or fight the tears anymore, so I sat snuggled up to the window and cried for the remaining three hours wondering...

What was wrong with me?
Why couldn't I stop crying?
What is life going to be like?
Will sound enter this silence that is so silent?

I had no control, so I had to just be!

Losing my father as a young adult, leaving toxic relationships, and making significant life changes, I thought I had mastered grieving. Yes, I indeed did and thought...

I will be able to get through and grieve this passing of mom. I know the routine; I have done it before. Piece of cake!

Everything happens for a reason. We moved Mom into her new home, which was not the location we wanted for long-term care. We managed to get her comfortable and worked on getting her to the place we desired. This was one of the most stressful events to have gone through. It was exactly a week later and the day before the move that she was admitted to the hospital.

It was surreal how were we living through this again so many years later but similar a journey; however, this was different.

I can only describe the experience as angelic, beautiful, and peaceful throughout, as hard as it was. Though we were not familiar with the hospital, the staff embraced us and made us feel like we were home as we moved into her room to be by her side. She told us she was tired of being in pain and right then I knew it was almost time. Calling family and friends, she was able to hear their kind words, and we were able to hear and feel all their love for her. She had lived an incredible life and inspired more people than we ever knew. We are so blessed that we were with both of our parents holding their hands at the moment of their last breath and able to say all we wanted to.

Knowing from experience, my logical mind told me we are going to move right through the seven stages of grief. I have been here before; I'm prepared; I've got this.

Well, grief had other plans for me, and I had no control over it. After I packed up the car after the funeral the next day, I drove through town and by my childhood home one last time. Having one more stop to make, I pulled slowly and quietly around the road to visit Mom and Dad at their final resting place. I got out of the car to say my final goodbyes, and that is where all things became so real.

I was not prepared to leave my parents behind and the town I grew up in. I did not expect to feel this final ending. This is it. I was not prepared for the silence that is so silent. For the first time in thirty-two years, I was only responsible for me and only me. There were no doctor calls, calling in a prescription, just calling to say hello, ordering groceries, going to appointments, or rushing off in the car for the three-hour drive to CT to visit Mom. No. Nope. Nothing. The silence was so silent.

When Dad passed, I was heartbroken—we had such a special bond, and he always provided the encouragement and support to be your best, help others, and live your life to the fullest. I helped Mom read up on the stages of grief, went to therapy, and kept moving forward. Being the oldest, I stepped in to help Mom navigate this new life and the loss of the love of her life. I didn't learn until I wrote my first book this year that I didn't grieve my dad. I suppressed this loss so far down that I filled the void with relationships and decisions that did not serve me well. Finally, after thirty-two years, I have grieved the loss of my father just in time to grieve the loss of my mother.

My life's journey has had incredible experiences, not-so-incredible ones, and everything in between. The last couple of years have been difficult for everyone. Close friends lost loved ones, lives changed, time was different, and we had to navigate this new world during the Covid-19 pandemic. Sharing my journey with the world during the pandemic and publishing the book, more relationships were removed from my life, and I have been able to understand more about my purpose and this new identity. But that is not all when I reflect—I realize that grief comes in many forms and at different times. Life events, identity changes and relationships also put you on the path to grieving. So logically you would think if you have been through it once before then it should be easier next time. Every situation is different and will take on its own path. Most importantly, let it be, just go with it and let it take its course.

I was brought up to be strong and confident and to never let anyone see me down. That last part—never let anyone see you down—was how I lived, and I did not allow myself to go through any grieving process for my dad, the loss of my identity, career changes or relationships.

But this process is still surprising me, and at times I feel like I was hit by that flying red gym ball we used in grade school to play dodgeball. I see it and feel it. I am at the center line with my opponent a few feet across from me and nowhere to go. I am hit with the speeding ball so hard I lose my breath and have the stinging burning pain of the ball hitting my skin. It is overwhelming.

I have felt physically ill, lost sleep, procrastinated, and literally walked and paced around the house. This is one area no one really talks about because we need to keep going. What I have realized is you need to have a balance. Let yourself be, listen to your body and take your time. Don't do what I did suppressing all the loss.

The same with the grieving process—it is overwhelming. Let it all out and be ok with asking for help. Cry, just cry, and give yourself some grace and be comfortable with just being.

What does this mean?

1. Don't be ashamed, all feelings are real;
2. It is ok to ask for help even with the simplest task;
3. Listen to your body, sleep when you need to, cry when you want, scream loud and let it all out;
4. Talk to someone. Be part of a group. You are not the only one going through this;
5. Do what you can—it will get done eventually;
6. There is no expiration date, so live in each moment and let it just be;
7. Don't listen to the noise around you. Be true to yourself;
8. Embrace the change at your pace. It is not a race;
9. Journal. It helps lift emotions and feelings from you;
10. Take time to care for yourself;
11. Release everything so it does not weigh you down;
12. Be yourself, be authentic, and share your thoughts and feelings;
13. Embrace the memories. Save the good, release and let go of the not-so-good;
14. Ground yourself;
15. Show up every day the best you can

This is still so fresh for me. It is difficult, it is emotional, and it is confusing. I have had days I am doing well and days I can't stop crying. There is a blank canvas in front of me and that scares me because I do not know how to navigate through this new world. I am staying grounded the best I can with consistent routines that I place in my day, but also giving myself leeway. Opening up and asking for help has always been a challenge for me because I know I can figure it out, but it is amazing if you ask for help how it actually makes a simple task easy and eliminates the stress and anxiety of getting it done. Asking for help is not being a failure; it is being real, and the more real you are the easier life is. We all have a purpose here, and I learned that through the legacy that was left by my mom.

My passion is helping people create personal and professional cultures, and I am on a mission to inspire, give hope and make an impact in people's lives and leave a legacy. Grieving any kind of loss is hard but it is part of our journey. Everything happens for a reason. Connect with me and together let's create your personal culture and navigate this new path.

ABOUT THE AUTHOR

Erin McCahill is a corporate leader, entrepreneur, mentor, innovator, personal and professional culture creator, and #1 International Best-Selling author. As a sales and customer experience leader in the tele-com, technology, and financial industry, she has built a strong repu-tation in building new organizations and revitalizing low-performing organizations while providing a superior customer expe-rience. Erin has received numerous awards in recognition of her success. She has found the passion that drives her: helping others build personal and professional cultures. Erin possesses a Bachelor of Science in business management and an MBA. Raised in Connecticut and now residing in southern New Jersey, Erin enjoys spending time with friends and family, sports, travel, entertaining, and planning events.

> **Website:** *www.themccahillgroup.com*
> **Facebook:** *www.facebook.com/erinamccahillmba*
> **LinkedIn:** *www.linkedin.com/in/erinamccahillmba*

CHAPTER FIVE

HOW TO PROPERLY SUPPORT A GRIEVER

GENEVA LIVINGSTONE

THE HARDEST DAY OF MY LIFE SINCE MY SON PASSED

I remember wanting to DO something REALLY, REALLY big on my son's birthday. By this time, we had lost two people eleven months apart, and we were completely unaware that two months after this video was recorded my family would lose another. Three in total..., My family experienced loss every eleven months for twenty-two months. My twenty-five- year- old son was the second.

I know you are most likely wondering WHY this was so hard? After all, it was in October. I managed to survive Easter, my birthday and even Mother's Day, but his birthday was beyond belief. As I sit writing this chapter, I feel EVERY emotion I felt that day. .This is why I decided to transcribe the video I did the next day...

My why is below...

The topic of the video was 5 Tips On Death Etiquette:

Firstly, before I even get into the five tips on death etiquette, I just want to thank you for the love and all of the support I get from all of you, my wonderful and amazing friends. Going through the passing of a loved one is hard, no matter who you are, and no matter the relationship, whether it is an aunt, an uncle, a child, a grown child, a cousin or a friend. If you guys had a bond, if you guys were close... it is Sweet Chaos, and it hurts regardless.

So the reason I am bringing up this conversation called Death Etiquette is that many of you may be friends of a person who is in mourning or going through a hard time, whether that person is in the hospital, in a coma or in the final stages of their lives. There isn't a book that tells you how to support that person, how to love that person through these things.

Like most situations, people draw in people who are in similar situations. During my time of loss, I was finding more women who had lost loved ones more than ever before. The bond wasn't just around the loss; it was around the support after the loss. We all came to the same consensus. This is where this conversation was born. I hope it will help you because it's not only about my voice but theirs voices too. These ideas hold the space for them and the things that they went through. We sit here knowing that these people love us but clearly don't know what to do.

So I think it's time..., Yesterday was my son's birthday., He would have been twenty-six. I had a very big huge plan—I was going to buy twenty-six helium balloons, and I was gonna let them go. And his baby was going to be there, and I was gonna do that with my family. And you know what, I woke up, and I couldn't, I just couldn't get out of bed. It was the hardest day. The absolute hardest day I went through, going to the hospital every day for twelve days. I survived Easter; I survived Mother's Day. But yesterday was the most taxing and the most empty I had felt since he passed. It was the weakest I've ever felt in this entire situation. And I was like, I'm gonna make this video and do all of these things, but I just couldn't. I couldn't do it.

I was talking to my mom about it and she said, "You know why it's a hard day? Because he was born and came into the world." So the impact of knowing that yesterday was the day that I kissed his head for the first time and remembering that I kissed his head until his body was cold at the hospital for the last time was just like a bit of a crowning glory in a way for me. So, this is the depth and the emotion of what that still feels like. So one of the things that are hard to hear when you are feeling like this is for somebody to say "over time, it will get better" (the tears are rolling down my cheeks at this moment).

Let's look inside. We want to scream and say to you, "I don't think so." So, etiquette tip number one, please don't say that. Because to the person's heart, it's like you're saying, "Maybe you're gonna forget the person." Now, I'm not saying that is what is being said, but I'm giving you our perspective of how it feels when it's translated into those emotions while in the emotional storm, or maybe you haven't made it far enough inside the storm yet. So please don't say that it really, really hurts..

The other thing is space. Culturally it may be where you are accustomed to having people come around you, and they're at your house every day. They just want to be there to support. But if you're not accustomed to that, having people in your home all the time while you're in the midst of these things is hard, because there's no barrier to what you have going on. And you have to,(I want to use the word entertain.) And I hope that you understand, what I'm saying is that you have to be on, you have to get up, you have to open the door... maybe you want to be in your lounge clothes all day, maybe you want to be in your bed all day,. but when people are coming around and that gathering is occurring, you have to do all of that, and that can wear you down inside. It takes a lot out of you.

Number three: When people in your circle hear that something has happened, they want to get in touch with you. Not a problem. They want to ask what happened? This is a hard question to answer. And again, this is just about adding guidance; it's not about you never asking, but in those moments, when you're like, "Oh, what happened? I'm sorry." You don't realize that you take the grieving person back into the emotion, back into the memories of all of that pain and hurt to explain it. If that person happens to have a very large support group, you'd be hearing the story for the first time while they've had to repeat that story over and over and over and over again. And it feels hard. It really really does. It's emotionally taxing. It might almost be easier to ask somebody around that circle. What happened? Because again, like I was saying, we live it again and again and again. And to have 50 People ask you is 50 times on top of your own emotions on top of your own hurt on top of your own pain on top of the storm that you're in the midst of.

Number four: We all mourn differently. For example, one lady that I was speaking to she was married, she lost her baby before he was a year old. She had carried him, nursed him, and changed his diapers, and before he made it to even a year, she lost him I think she lost him at around 11 months. When I was telling her I was going to do this, one of the things that came up from people around her was, "Well, you know, you don't really look like this situation just happened to you." And she was like, "Are you kidding me? Are you kidding me that people are saying this to me?" And the reason is that on top of having this new baby, she also had a small child at home and a husband. And as a wife and mother, all she could say was, "If I break down right now, is it going to bring my baby back?" Because there is an expectation of how you're supposed to feel or how you're supposed to look or where your emotions are supposed to go. She didn't want to be that mom that wasn't there for her small child. She didn't want to be that wife that wasn't there for her husband, who was also having a hard time losing his son, especially since he did not have the opportunity to even be there. So she had a lot on her plate. And people were calling and were upset, and they're crying. And I understand that you may want to share this, I get it, I get it, I get it. Your friends cry when you cry; they laugh when you laugh. They rejoice when you rejoice, and they're in pain when you're in pain. But sometimes, the pain that you as a support person are going through when you place the weight on somebody who already feels like they can't take any more, they feel like they have to hold it together for others. That's hard. That's so hard.

My fifth tip—and this is the tip of freedom—is to just ask. How can I support you? What do you need? Knowing that you have all of those people, I use 50. Because it's an easy number, but knowing that you have all those people that if it was like that lady that was talking to me about her husband and her small child support for her would have been listening, if you have a day and you can't get out of bed, you call me. Because I know that it means I need to be there, so you can take that day to yourself or that hour to yourself or those minutes to yourself.

My friend asked, "What can I do for you? Is it coming to clean for you? Well, you don't have to think about that. Is it preparing a meal? Is it just me sitting there with you on the couch? Not even talking but just being present?" The asking is the most powerful tool that you as a support person can give to a person that's going through this. Yes, we want the love and care. But because each of us is different, we need it differently.

And I'm just gonna throw in this little bit of a bonus.

The normal human instinct is to grab us, you know?

And as much as I am a loving huggy type of person, it was the last thing I wanted when all this was happening. It was the very last thing I wanted. So I guess I'm just saying that as a person in the midst of it, and again, with people that I've spoken to, who have gone through this, who are in the motion of going through it, just ask. There's so much freedom. And then let the person tell you how you can best support them. And please, please, please do not be offended if what they want is not what you were prepared to give or isn't what you thought they needed. It is a hard road. And there are no rules, there simply are none.

But the situation sometimes can make it hard for us to see very good perspectives on both sides for the supporter and the mourner. So I just wanted to make this video called Death Etiquette, five tips. And I know I ended with six. And thank you for reading. I appreciate all of you. And if you know somebody who is having that hard time, before you react in any way, the best and most amazing thing that you can do is ask these simple questions. How can I support you? What do you need? And then the second thing for yourself is being okay with whatever that answer turns out to be. And again, I want to thank you and let you know how much my family, and I appreciate all the support, all the love and all the care that we received and still continue to receive during this period, and I'm hoping that it's my only storm for a long time—but my greatest storm.

I hope that this shared moment somehow changes either how you as a griever show up for yourself or how you might show up the next time someone around you experiences loss.

While I wrote this chapter, this video was just one small moment but it was my most raw.

May the hearts of all those that allowed me to give them a voice be heard, loved and cared for be beautifully full.

P.S If you would like a copy of the actual video, please message me at the website in my bio.

Grief, Fire & Hope,
Geneva Coach G Livingstone

ABOUT THE AUTHOR

Geneva Livingstone is a compressed grief survivor. This means that three mothers in a short twenty-two-month period were forced to say goodbye to their children. For Geneva, this meant saying goodbye to her one and only son Nathaniel at the age of twenty-five.

Each person's passing was exactly eleven months apart, and when she lost her second cousin, Geneva was soooo fed up with loss that she turned her anger into passion and decided to open an Instagram account that focused on loss.... not just her own but the loss of loved ones for others. Her account includes parental, partner, and child loss. She is so determined not to leave anyone behind.

Instead of only sharing her own story and helping hearts through that,. Geneva went on to become a Certified Master Life & Grief Coach and well as a Confident Grief Coach. With her passionate down-to-earth nature, she really just prefers to be called Coach G 😊...

As a Compassionate Leader in Grief, she feels it's her heart's song to light the path of grief for others by guiding them to discover how to masterfully master their lives, their grief and their happiness...

Website: www.m.me/geneva.coachg.livingstone

CHAPTER SIX

GRIEF'S UNFORESEEN INVITATION

KARLYN LANGJAHR

"Where are you from?" I'm asked, in a predictable fashion following the standard name exchange.

I t should be a straightforward, harmless question, but it leaves me doubting myself. I'm stung with insecurity because of how much I've moved around, despite always having been open to settling down in one of the many homes I've been lucky to land in.

As much as I pride myself on the diverse range of cultures, geographies and "adventures" I've taken in from an unintentionally nomadic lifestyle, deep down there's an unsettled ping of "What's wrong with me? Why can't I make a residence work out somewhere?"

Sometimes I don't know where I'm from anymore; my birth home of Wisconsin never felt like my true "home". At the same time, I feel like I carry every place I've lived in within me.

So why can't I just simply and truthfully reply, "I was born and raised in Wisconsin but have lived all over the world."?

Out comes an awkward laugh as I try to hide how oddly uncomfortable this question makes me: "Planet Earth, basically."

~

If you would have known me before my husband's devastating suicide, you would have felt a free-spirited woman following her passions and living out her dream, working in wildlife conservation in one of the most spectacular ecosystems in Africa, if not the world. My life was rich in relationships and connection in community and the environment. I had a circle of cherished friends from across the globe who I'd known during any of my various home bases: Wisconsin, France, Panama, New Mexico, Washington State, U.S. Virgin Islands, Zanzibar, Costa Rica, and Zambia (not including personal or professional trip destinations). Before writing this chapter from New Mexico, I would add Wyoming and Mexico to the list.

A young-at-heart forty-something, you would have also picked up on my ability to see the good in (nearly) anyone and realistic optimism—or at least hope—which were the results of my natural inclination coupled with nearly twenty years of meditation and yoga practices.

Not to mention a lifetime of presenting myself in a polished way.

Admittedly, that's how I stayed with my husband through the cumulative years of his increasingly dark view of himself and the world. Part of me held on to how bright and sparky his inner light was thirteen years ago and believed he would find it again. Sometimes the glimmers of his shiny core would flicker out again, and I thought if I just loved him more he would see how lovable he was.

What you wouldn't have seen... the bouts of anxiety that riddled me, the stomach burn and tightness I woke up to, or even the occasional panic attacks that only Cam was privy to witnessing.

You wouldn't have seen the accumulated toll that perfectionism and people-pleasing had on me or felt the crushing weight of pressure I put on myself. You wouldn't have known that I considered myself a "failure" in so many ways, even though my life was really good.

I wasn't aware of it at the time, but I so deeply longed for a sense of stability and belonging that I never felt from my birth home, family, or classmates.

Don't we all just desire acknowledgment and a sense of belonging?

For me, external validation was sought through the praise of my bosses or coworkers, compliments from my yoga students, affection and time from my husband and step-daughter, the likes and comments received by friends and "friends" on my posts on social and in real life, etc.

Even though I was satisfied with my direction in life, I never felt like what I did was "good enough". (The never-ending "to-do" list keeps you in a state of urgency and hypervigilance- you can't go on vacation without thinking of the stress of opening the inbox upon return, so you check it while you're supposed to be "checked out").

In spite of all my hard work, kindness and genuineness, my career was anything but financially sustainable.

I quixotically hoped that the appreciation and acknowledgment would make up for the lackluster salary and lack of insurance, pension or other "real job" benefits. Of course, there exist well-paid conservation careers with benefits, oftentimes in undesirable (to me) cities with corporate-like offices and work pace, but I never believed I could even land one of them. Or that I could choose such an environment, away from the nature that drew me to the profession in the first place.

I figured that "one day" I would reach long-term prosperity and somehow pay off my hefty student loans and have health insurance, pension and decent paid time off. I didn't have the traditional desires of buying a house, owning a fancy car or having biological kids; I just wanted a solid work-life balance.

Even though I had somewhat resigned myself to the fact that I might be a perpetual planktonic drifter, deep down there was an unadopted desire to anchor into a community on a long-term basis. Because it was so foreign to me and somehow out of reach, I instead created the belief that my connections constituted "home" for me, and that was sufficient.

Friends, more like "chosen family", provided the sense of community I longed for in my adult life, in addition to nature and wildlife. I accepted that I didn't "have to" identify with or pinpoint a geographical home in this lifetime as an Earthling, as long as I could carry my chosen family with me in my heart wherever I went.

Just because we're capable of something doesn't mean it's what we truly desire for ourselves.

In addition to my lack of sense of belonging or "home-ness" to a particular place on Earth, I lived with Cam's inability to feel completely "at home" on Earth, in the human experience. He didn't even feel at home in his body, plagued by chronic back and body pain; he often remarked how "home" to him was with me, and that there was no better feeling than when we cuddled up together with my head resting on his chest. It was our way of grounding and recalibrating, even when friction coursed through our communication.

A few weeks before he plummeted to his death in the crocodile-rich Luangwa River, Cam asked me, "Do you love yourself?" with genuine inquisitiveness. I paused, a bit taken aback by the lightness in tone, because our conversation leading up to that moment was dense with discord between our differing outlooks, his glass-half-empty heightened by his deteriorating self-esteem.

"No," I carefully considered his question, "but I'm getting closer. I don't know if I'll ever fully get there, but I mostly like who I am."

What came out of his mouth next showed me how dark of a place he was in: "I don't even like myself. I hate myself..." to which I didn't even have a reply. I didn't have time to, either, because we had just reached his drop-off point where he abruptly hopped out of the vehicle and skirted away before I could utter much more than a "see you later..." and continued onward to my office.

Things I adored about Cam: he approached everything he did with an artistic eye (even in how he chose to end his life); his creative perspective opened others' view of the world; his uncanny way of giving permission for others to be unabashedly themselves. Cam jested that he believed in "everything and nothing" at the same time —it was all just belief. When asked what his favorite flavor of ice cream was, he would matter-of-factly retort, "Whatever flavor I'm having right now," because he could be that present in a moment of pleasure.

Although Cam was worldly and internationally adaptable to many places he lived in or visited, he prided himself on his Midwestern upbringing known for its strong work ethic and family values. Cam had a much deeper sense of rootedness to the region we were both raised in; I often envied that about him and wished I felt that same pull to my birth home. I said I was the black sheep of my family; in a quirky fashion, he countered that he was the purple sheep of his.

Equally an artist and handy man, I appreciated Cam's attention to detail and innovation. He crafted from a mechanical methodology that both impressed and bored me; it was seriously a shame he had given up on landing a profession where he felt he could marry his knowledge, passions and skill sets. Honestly, his ideal job was a stay-at-home dad tending to all of the tedious errands and logistics I dreaded and avoided. Yet my job didn't financially provide that as an option, and we only spent summer and winter breaks with his beloved daughter.

Over time, this sense of purposelessness, inability to be a

provider like the patriarchal system dictates for males, and distance to his daughter (physical and later emotional) drove him into an irreconcilable depression.

But no one knew me better or loved me as fully as Cam did. To meet someone who "gets" you so completely is one of the greatest gifts in humankind, and one I will never take for granted.

Ultimately, we can only meet someone at the level we've met ourselves, however.

I knew grief would be a long, meandering journey, like a river. I was very prepared for the massive ebbs and flows and to feel all the feels. For what control do the river banks have over the timeless power of water forces carving their path to the sea?

When we zoom out, we see how all of the channels are linked, essentially flowing as one entity, even as they expand, contract, and morph.

What I didn't foresee was the portal of grief to surrendering, not in the sense of giving away my power but giving into my own inner power. And in the least expected of places.

Five months after Cam's death, I returned "home" to the U.S. for the first time in two and a half years. I wanted to continue living and working in Zambia, but I couldn't bring myself to stay on any longer.

I thought taking another healing trip to my favorite country of Madagascar with my favorite animals (lemurs) would re-center and re-inspire me. Instead, I was left with a profound sense of disorientation and an overwhelming feeling of "I just want to go *home*." Except that I had no idea where home was anymore.

Did I ever, truly? I didn't even feel like I belonged in the glorious Luangwa Valley any longer, as much as I wanted to linger in the space where Cam's molecules were recycled back into the abundant wildlife. My first true loves, wildlife and Cam. Maybe that's what I had espoused as "home"?

It wasn't a sense of physical homelessness, with countless offers from family and friends to regroup in their lovely abodes.

My take-"home" (pun intended) sentiment was how inherently connected I was to a greater force that was bigger than myself; a deep remembrance that my own unique energetic blueprint was a fractal of divine Source Energy.

But how to ground that back into my human experience and live out that knowing as an Earthling? Especially at a time that felt both insignificant in the grand scheme and wildly transformational at the same time?

Upon my return stateside, it also hit me why I had been drawn to the beauty and cultures of other countries since high school. As an outsider, I was often so warmly welcomed and embraced. It was both startling and refreshing to receive that amount of attention, because I had never felt so seen. This was quite the contrast as a middle child buried in the pack of my blended family of five siblings. As a thirteen-month-old, I also had my spotlight prematurely stolen from me when my brother entered the world (much to the amiss of my Moon in Leo).

I was fortunate to catch the travel bug at an early age, especially since my parents were so supportive of me pursuing my interests and the fact that my studies and professional endeavors carried me abroad. The more I ventured out and witnessed new ways of life, the more curious I became to other perspectives, even if they clashed with my own values, because I didn't take them on as I would have with the predominant way of life in the USA. My detachment from them is ironically what allowed me to connect more deeply to them.

Truthfully, I was far more critical toward my home country

because I felt that we had the resources and intelligence to create a society that worked for the greater good, but that we were too greedy and materialistic. It was easier to adopt a more forgiving attitude toward less privileged lands since they seemed to have greater uphill battles with corruption, human rights and access to education.

Over time, I felt more distant from my identity as an American even though it was my "home" nationality. I always preferred to consider myself a citizen of the world, aka Earthling.

Although I only planned for a return trip to the U.S. as a launch pad for healing resources and time with my loving and supportive family, Covid quashed my hopes to relocate internationally again.

I jumped on the invitation from my best friend to live in Wyoming, which ended up being one of the biggest blessings in disguise for me. I had never moved somewhere without first having a job and didn't know how long I would end up there. I also had no idea how much of a gift that period of time in those lands would be, not just in terms of appreciating my birth country on a whole new level, but also re-finding aspects of myself and joys that I neglected for decades due to all of the ways I thought I "should" be.

We often hear, "the grass is greener on the other side," when really the grass is greener where we water it, and what a surprise it was to water the proverbial grasses in the high desert surrounded by three mountain ranges.

I had no idea how much 2020 would become a homecoming for me personally: coming home to myself, the result of taking a sacred pause during the global pandemic to surrender to even more uncertainties of life.

Before leaving Zambia, I came across a beautiful natural history quote that sparked hope about my next chapter in life, particularly since I had been so torn about leaving that beautiful and wild community I had cherished so deeply: "*observation of the wren's propensity to migrate has led to man's realization that home can be anywhere, as long as there is love.*" I let that sink in.

I knew I had it within me to uproot myself again because I have done it over and over before; I just didn't know that I was about to unexpectedly make the best, and hardest, move ever in my life: the move inward to my true self.

In spite of Cam's absence as well as our sometimes complex relationship, it was also true for me that love itself never ever dies and that love is worth celebrating however much it hurts. I determined that Cam would live on through me by how I carried on with the impact he made on me in my heart.

While I never expected to find a home within myself in Wyoming of all places, I expected even less to find love again there, which is what happened when naturally exuding my newfound peace, acceptance and joy. Our relationship arose organically and unexpectedly after spending time and sharing conversations over mutual recreational passions in the great outdoors. It was a love nurtured from genuine ease, respect and teamwork and evolved steadily. We found ourselves talking about future plans, calling his dog and van "ours", dreaming up adventures while I launched my online business, and he prepared to wind down in his profession.

Alas, our partnership ended up having a shelf life of fourteen beautiful months with the warmest split possible. As our visions subsequently crumbled, it led me to another re-examination of "home" in terms of my sense of identity and relationship to that place.

Naturally, another wave of grief swept in as I also mourned the loss of endless possibilities that love makes us feel capable of. Yet I knew I carried home within me wherever I went. After living in remote, land-locked river ecosystems for four consecutive years, I was called back to my first love of the ocean and let myself be carried to that pull. I set out to explore making a new community for myself in a dream town on Mexico's Central Pacific coast.

Privy to the independence that singlehood affords, I went all in on my business. I allowed myself to be fully me, including the mysticism, in building long-term self-sufficiency for the first time in my life. I claimed my gifts, stepped into my leadership and showed up in my authority.

And WOW, did I find everything I set out for: soul-family and spiritual connections, an abundance of lush nature both from the sea and jungles, an open-hearted culture based on appreciation for artistic and creative endeavors.

It was an absolutely magical place where the epiphany dropped in that I truly desire a permanent home base, and it wouldn't be there. I leaned into my deeper place of self-trust and pursued the inner guidance, synchronicities and dreams that led me to New Mexico, where I'm now building the life of my ultimate vision.

Home for me is radical self-acceptance, no matter where I am or what I'm moving through. It's my ability to show up for myself no matter what I'm feeling, both wanted and unwanted emotions, and to acknowledge each one equally, without aversion or attachment.

"Home can be anywhere, as long as there is love."

Life shows us that humanity can be brutal, unfair and full of suffering. Yet it also reveals beauty, love and lessons to us over and over again. What are we going to choose? Can that simple choice in itself change the world for the better?

That's my belief: that in celebrating and loving life every single day, we are transforming Earth.

While it is all still in process of creation, it's already coming together beautifully. The embodiment of home within me allows me to anchor more solidly into my physical space.

Home is wherever I go because I fully accept and love myself.

So here I am at home. For the first time in my life, I feel at home both internally and in my physical environment.

If the only legacy I leave behind in this lifetime is unconditional love and showing others that it's possible to lead from that place, I will have fulfilled my heart's greatest desire.

ABOUT THE AUTHOR

Karlyn Langjahr is a spiritual life coach, healer and author who draws upon her passion for nature and her previous career as a wildlife conservationist.

After losing her husband, Cam, to suicide in 2019 while living in Zambia, she dove even further into her life's purpose and how to make the biggest impact with her remaining time on Earth. Her loss jolted her onto a rich journey of coming home to herself after having lived and traveled all over the world. This has been the most profound gift in her life.

Karlyn's grief journey was a portal to surrendering her need to plan out her life based on who she thought she had to be. She now guides ambitious leaders and perfectionists to release the grip of control over their lives and create success based on how they are feeling instead of just by what they do or have. She infuses movement, energy work, ceremony, sacred space and the wisdom and spirits of nature into her offerings.

Karlyn is cherished for her non-judgmental and open heart, authenticity, vulnerability and willingness to choose love and courage over fear, again and again.

Instagram: www.instagram.com/karlyn_langjahr
Facebook: www.facebook.com/karlyn.langjahr
Website: www.karlyn.langjahr

2
ANGELS, THEIR MAMAS AND MIRACLES

MALAINE LEAH BUTLER
&
GEORGIA HANSEN

GEORGIE, MAY 2021

I took a few deep breaths; grounded and anchored myself; set the intention that whatever she needs to hear for her highest good will come through. I never know what state an angel mama will be in when I connect with her for the first time.

I dialled her number. When she answered, her voice was so sweet, her New Jersey drawl was noticeable in the first few words, and oh so endearing.

I was driving, and I distinctly remember where I was on the road when I had the feeling that I had finally found the one I'd been waiting for.

Months earlier, I had sent out a honing beacon to the Universe and asked for them to bring me a partner—someone who understood my journey and who got it at the level that I did.

And here she was, packaged in a woman whose baby had only just died days earlier.

Her name was Malaine. A mutual friend who I didn't know all that well had reached out to me to ask if I would be willing to chat to her as her baby boy Noah had died and she had asked her community if there was anyone she could talk to.

Within minutes, I knew she was the one who I'd be sharing my mission with.

We both felt it. Even though she was only days into her grief journey. We both knew there was something big and magical at play.

MALAINE AND NOAH

May 18th 2021 is the day my baby's heart stopped beating. To be honest, for a moment it felt like my heart stopped beating too.

The day started like every day in my pregnancy with my sweet son Noah Alexander. I woke up, had my breakfast, and started my work day. At 1 pm, I had a scheduled midwife appointment for my birthing plan, I was thirty-seven weeks pregnant. My doula and I arrived a little early to the appointment so we chatted in the waiting room. We laughed about how the labour would go and what Noah would be like. My midwife came out into the waiting room to get us, greeting us both with a smile and a hug. After an hour of chatting about my birthing plan, my midwife asked me to hop on the table to check the heartbeat of my baby.

After a few minutes, it was clear she couldn't find it. Calmly, she invited in another midwife who also, after several minutes, found nothing. They then brought me into a special room with a monitor to do a bedside scan. In that moment, I knew Noah had died. Their faces told the story before they even uttered a word. Instead of confirming Noah had died, they said, "lets get you to the hospital to see what exactly is going on."

En route to the hospital I whispered to Noah, fighting back my tears, "Noah, my love, kick for mummy, kick for mummy." As the short ride, which felt like eternity, neared the end, I knew the truth... Noah was dead. My husband Ryan met me at the hospital. As he entered the room my whole body was shaking. I lay down as they prepped me for yet another scan. Then they said the dreaded words...

"I am so sorry we cannot find a heartbeat."

My husband screamed in agony. He shouted. "Find the heartbeat! This is my son. He is thirty-seven weeks. This cannot be happening!"

The midwife calmly said, "I am so sorry sir he has passed away."

We headed to another "more professional" scan in another wing of the hospital to officially confirm Noah's death. The woman said, "yes I can confirm your son has died."

I looked at my husband and burst into tears. In that exact moment 4:06 pm on May 18th, the old Malaine died forever... never to return.

Crossing the threshold of the doorway back into the maternity ward I emerged another woman. A different woman. One who would never be privy to life without child loss. One that would never be blind to the tragedy that can occur. From that day forward, my life was split in two. The one before Noah's death and the one after.

Two days later I was back at the same hospital to be induced and give birth to my forever third son, Noah. The dream of my at-home water birth, gone. The dream of completing my family of all boys, gone. And instead emerged new dreams, new desires and a new normal way of living.

Noah's birth was, quite honestly, the most sacred birth of all my boys. It was magical. Yes, there was pain, sorrow, grief, and sadness BUT there was also beauty, divinity and true love present. After five hours of natural labor with minimal pain relief, he was born vaginally with ease.

Noah was born at 10:53 pm on May 20th 2021. Instead of the loud cries, he was silent. The room was silent. My midwife whispered softly to me, "He's here Malaine, Noah is here." She wrapped him in a cloth and laid him on my chest. I didn't cry. I said over and over again, "Noah I just love you so much. So much Noah. I love you so so much." My husband gently rubbed my arm and put his hand on Noah. He said softly, "our son is perfect, he looks just like his brothers."

He was perfect. The most beautiful face, nose, hands, and feet. He looked just like my other two boys. We call them triplets.

Noah was born with the umbilical cord wrapped tightly around his neck several times. The compression stopped the flow of all nourishment he needed. Later tests confirmed the conclusion that he died from the cord accident.

Since his heart stopped beating my life has changed irrevocably.

Noah gave me permission to live life exactly how I desire. He showed me the vibrancy the world has to offer. He gave me an understanding of gratitude and appreciation for my children.

A little over a year after Noah died, Ava Marie Butler was born. Ava means life and Marie means desired child.

Ava is by no means a replacement, but she is mending our hearts and bringing new life back into our home.

Noah was meant to be our last child. When he died we decided to have one more. So we named his little sister Ava because we believe he is the reason she has life.

Yes, Noah died. It was the worst day of my entire existence. And I can't change what has happened. So I have chosen to LIVE because of Noah not in spite of the experience. I've chosen to live because of and for my son. Noah's legacy lives on through me, through my family.

GEORGIE AND AMELIA

Amelia was baby number four in our family. She followed three little boys. She was so long-awaited and her brothers, daddy and I were beyond excited for her arrival. After all, we had known of her existence since I had first dreamed of her eight years earlier. In that dream, I was clearly shown her name *Amelia Jade* written out in chalk on a driveway. I would then "see" her in the faces of random little girls with curly blonde hair out in the world. Often, when my head would turn involuntarily to see a little girl standing with her family, smiling and staring back at me, I'd be left with this notion that the Universe was handing me a signal.

We knew she was coming. It was just a matter of *when*. Finally, after eight years of waiting, I told my husband she was ready to come. He knew by now to trust me. That same month we conceived her. Fast forward to July 27, 2017, one day over her due date. I was finally on the way to the hospital in *very* active labour. We were ready to meet the soul we had so long waited for. In hindsight, I should have felt excited about our dream finally coming true. The only way I can describe the feeling I had en route to the hospital was an emptiness and a feeling of doom.

We pulled up and rushed into the Pregnancy Assessment Unit. As we were led into the consultation room, I was contracting with only a ten to thirty-second break in between. I told the midwife I was hoping for a water birth, and she started getting that ready with the other birth-suite staff.

She came back in with a doppler (a monitor that gets placed on the mother's belly to detect the baby's heart rate), and while I was fully focused on breathing through the intensity of the contractions, she put the machine on my bump to trace a heartbeat. I was standing and contracting powerfully, so after a few minutes of her not being able to find a heartbeat, I wasn't concerned. After a few minutes, she decided to call in the Registrar doctor with a scanner. The doctor came in. The midwife stood to my left, with the doctor to my right, with the medical scanner facing towards both of them. My husband sat on a chair next to me. All three displayed meek, poker faces.

Another few seconds of silence passed, and the Registrar said she was going to get a more senior doctor. The next doctor came in and started scanning. I was still strangely calm. I looked at the first doctor who stood at the foot of the bed, and I remember so clearly how she slowly pulled out what looked like a walkie-talkie and held it close to her face. That was the moment I knew something was wrong and everything slowed to a standstill. Time, space and the very air in the room seemed to disappear. The excruciating labour pain seemed non-existent for those few seconds. I blurted out loudly, "What's going on?", and that's when the second doctor put her hand on my knee and told me, "I'm so sorry, there is no heartbeat."

This is the moment that changed my life forever. "I'm so sorry darling, she's gone," she said matter-of-factly. "What do you mean? She's right there. Look at my belly, she's right there. Find her!" I yelled, as if they were talking about something they had lost in the forest. Now there was another doctor in the room. A man, this time. Maybe he could find her, I thought. His words to me were soft and kind, but very firm. She was gone.

You hear stories of primal screams when a mother loses her young in the wild. I have come to learn humans are no different. Even in the confines of the most pristine manmade settings, we are in essence wild, free animals. In those first moments, I made sounds I had never heard come out of my, or any other human's, mouth. I hope I never hear them again. Those raging, primitive noises were followed by the most extraordinary experience of my life. A vibration entered my body. I now know it to be the highest vibration there is; *Universal Source Energy* or *God*. It reverberated through every cell in my being! It still echoes in my ear when I recall it loudly saying, "Everything is actually going to be okay!" Somehow, I trusted it to be true. I went on to deliver the most divine baby girl. She was blonde with gorgeous lips and round cheeks. She was the most beautiful angel, full of Grace, beauty and magic. Everything about her was perfect. Everything, except for the stillness.

I can recall every second of every minute of every hour that followed for the next twenty-four hours. We got to spend the next few hours holding her, crying together and adoring every inch of her small body. My husband bathed her with the midwife, and the midwife dressed her in the first of two outfits she would ever wear. Holding my baby girl, I stared in wonder at her perfection. I wept and wondered why? I questioned everything, including what I could have done to have caused this. It was such a surreal feeling both wanting to hold this baby forever, and at the same time wanting to be so far away.

Every moment of my life since has been a reaction to the catalytic event that altered my life. I vow to live a life of *Grace*, reverence and beauty in honour of my daughter. Further, to teach and be an exemplar who shows others there is magic in absolutely everything. Even and especially, in the tragic.

BIRTH OF ANGEL MAMA HOUSE

When we met, it was kismet. We had met many other Angel Mamas, some of whom had become lifelong friends, but we yearned for more.

We knew there was a segment of humanity suffering in silence, with very little to no support in helping them to actually heal. We knew Grace to be found in Grief, and Magic in the tragic.

Our journeys have shown us power, strength and magic beyond what we thought was possible. They have also changed our perception of life. We can see the beauty that surrounds us in every single moment, and every day we choose to show up. We show up for the lows to feel them and to move through them. Please don't quash those intense and raw emotions. For once you move through those lows, you will feel those magical highs.

The trauma and grief recovery we walked didn't include a single antidepressant drug (even though we have unashamedly used them in the past), nor a single appointment with a psychologist (despite having benefited from therapy previously). We dove even further into personal development, learned various healing modalities, and trained in intuitive sciences, universal laws and quantum physics. We gathered and curated resources. We did the work on the inside and found what we needed *within us*. We dug deep into our souls and examined every inch. We were readying ourselves.

Nothing like what we needed existed when we lost our babies.

So we gathered all of the tools, resources, knowledge and

wisdom that was channelled to us from the Divine to create a safe haven for other women like us.

God had handed us a mission.

ANGEL MAMA HOUSE

A sanctuary for warrior women who've experienced miscarriage, stillbirth or infant loss.

A sacred hub with a membership community. We are starting with a twelve-month framework for walking through grief, and there are big plans to add more programs, in-person events, workshops, and retreats, as well as resources, books and products.

We want to create a thriving global community. A safe space for warrior women who've experienced loss to feel seen, heard, and supported. A community to come home to, to find solace, safety, connection and guidance.

We want to show others facing a loss of this magnitude to live in the state of being that knows it's possible to not only survive following the unfathomable loss of a child but to thrive. It is possible to live a beautiful life, not in spite of losing our babies, but because of them!

The truth is, we believe the Universe doesn't give us these experiences to punish or destroy us. Rather, it shows what we are capable of in service of our growth. Our *Light* is our ability to love unconditionally, no matter how broken our heart is. To love with compassion, and to forgive, for when we know this power, we know the blessing of what it's truly like to be alive. We will never ever take that for granted.

As Einstein said, "you can live your life as if nothing is a miracle, or as if everything is". We choose to believe in the latter.

ABOUT THE AUTHORS

Malaine Leah Butler is a master coach and transformational business owner serving purpose-driven mothers to transform their business so that they can prioritize family and a life of financial freedom. She has been running her coaching practice for eight years and has served thousands of people in transforming, expanding and upleveling their lives. Recently, Malaine completed her doula certification to allow her to support angel mothers in their journey of pregnancy after loss. Malaine has been featured in Money INC, Huffington Post, Life Coach Magazine, Addicted to Success Podcast, Elephant Journal, Spiritual Awakening Podcast, and Entrepreneur INC. When Malaine is not serving her clients, she is being a mother to Jack, Liam, Ava, stepson Cameron, angel mother to Noah, shopping with a mocha in hand or hanging with her husband in Auckland, NZ.

Learn more about Malaine and Angel Mama House at:
Website: *www.angelmamahouse.com*

ABOUT THE AUTHORS

Georgia (aka Georgie) Hansen is an eclectic mix of PR, marketing communications savvy, and soulful intuitive wisdom with a deep understanding of human communication, collaboration, and connection.

She is trained as a transformational intuitive guide and priestess of non-local consciousness who is trauma-informed and embodied. She uses this along with her communications, PR and publishing expertise to look through the cracks and help women connect with their highest self and purpose, especially angel mamas who are seeking to find meaning after loss. Georgie helps them to find the beauty, and wonder in their story, and shines a light on it.

Georgie is an international best-selling author and publisher and has been featured on various podcasts, summits, and events and published in top-tier National publications.

She lives in sunny Queensland, Australia, with her twin flame hubby and her four earth-side babes Breyten, Toby, Eli and Amber. And her heart is stretched to reach her angel baby Amelia in Heaven. She has a powerful story, message, and mission to shift a paradigm around loss, grief, trauma, and tragedy. She teaches there is grace and magic to be found in it all.

Learn more about Georgia and Angel Mama House at:
Website: *www.angelmamahouse.com*

CHAPTER EIGHT

CHARLOTTE

MARIANNE YOUNG

Two dates changed my life forever: the day my granddaughter
Charlotte was born and the day she died.

C harlotte entered this world six weeks early, weighing
just 3 lbs. 2 oz. She was a tiny miracle. We met when
she was an hour old. I put my finger into her incubator to
say hello and five tiny perfect fingers wrapped around my fingernail.
In that moment Charlotte tucked herself into my heart and our
amazing, unbreakable bond began.

We learned shortly after her birth that she was born with a rare
disease known as Wolf Hirschhorn or 4p- (named for the gene that
partially deleted during conception). The doctors said Charlotte
would be delayed in nearly every developmental process. I believed
our tiny earth angel would show everyone she could do more than
they expected. Charlotte was little but mighty; she was our Warrior
Princess and knew how to fight for life. She battled so many
extended hospital visits throughout her short life. In December 2017,
she was just 3 ½ months old and was hospitalized with RSV, bron-
chitis, and coronavirus. She fought it all and made it home for her

first Christmas. I remember one of her first views of her Christmas tree. I was holding her on my lap, and she was fascinated by the lights on the tree. She raised her sweet little hand and reached for the lights. When she couldn't touch them, she sighed but kept watching the beautiful light show. Charlotte and I truly enjoyed those moments—it was Christmas magic.

The next big battle was Charlotte's open-heart surgery when she was eight months old (weighing just 8 lbs.). Just hours after surgery she was looking for all of us. We were able to visit and comfort her. She came through with flying colors. As the months went on, Charlotte endured so many seizures that came with her rare disease. She had such a sweet personality that nothing kept her down. She always bounced back. She was well-loved at the Children's Hospital of Philadelphia (CHOP). The nurses used to braid her hair and rock her to sleep. Everyone who met Charlotte was amazed by the big personality this little lady had.

As time went on, Charlotte had such awful reflux that she couldn't tolerate digesting food, so she was finally given a permanent GJ tube for feeding. She was hooked up to liquid feedings through her GJ tube while being slowly fed for twenty out of every twenty-four hours and then given a four-hour break to allow time for her body to rest. Charlotte came through everything until she turned two and had a major cardiac arrest. She was down for seventeen minutes. They saved her, but she gained a new issue: brain damage. Now the doctors said Charlotte would never walk, talk, crawl or be able to progress as she would have. She was placed in palliative care at her home. The doctors weren't sure she would live long after what she had suffered. I again believed in our girl. I would tell Charlotte that she was strong and amazing and that the choices were hers. I told her she could do anything she wanted to. She always listened attentively to me. She understood what I said to her. She may have been non-verbal, but she understood and could communicate if you paid attention to her unique ways. I never left our visits without telling her how much I loved her and how special she was to me.

Charlotte was truly one of the greatest loves of my life. Holding her was heaven for me. I never wanted to put her down. I know she felt my love just as I felt hers. Charlotte loved to snuggle in and take a nap with me. She was so warm; we'd both usually end up napping for a while.

In the summer of 2021, Charlotte went along on her mother's family vacation to Tennessee. I had a sickness in the pit of my stomach because I worried she would get COVID. When they came home, my son delivered the news I had been fearing: Charlotte had contracted COVID. The next three weeks, Matt and Charlotte lived at CHOP. We weren't sure if she could beat this. Thankfully God wasn't ready for her, so she came home to her family and life went on. Charlotte now needed oxygen much more than she used to. I was so happy we still had our girl. I loved the way she'd look into my eyes. Her sweet, quiet love filled my heart and soul with a joy I've never experienced and may never know again. We had such a mutual love and understanding we never needed words. I always prayed with Charlotte. I always thanked God for keeping her alive and healing her. I knew this sweet girl was a gift to all of us. I cherished the gift of her life and enjoyed every moment with her.

Christmas 2021 was very special. I made Charlotte a special blanket with pictures of both of us. I also put the words to our song on the blanket "When You Say Nothing at All." On the inside of the blanket, I used material with a giraffe pattern (her favorite). Charlotte's eyes lit up when I gave her the blanket. This was us, our story. I never knew the blanket I gave her last Christmas would be back with me within six months.

The beginning of 2022 was not good. I will leave the details out for the privacy of Charlotte's parents. I was unable to visit since things were very tense. On Father's Day June 19, 2022, I got a call from my son saying Charlotte had just days to live. She had pneumonia and the medicines were not helping. I was invited to visit with many of the family members that day. I held Charlotte close as I always did. I had to try to memorize her face, the smell of her hair, the softness of her skin; all the things I always tried to memorize in case this day ever came. I knew this was goodbye. I had no idea how I would live in a world without Charlotte. Charlotte was medicated for pain and sleeping peacefully. She tried to open her eyes for me, but I told her to rest. I rocked her gently and sang our song to her through my tears.

Monday, I went to work and heard she was still with us, her breathing grew shallower. My older son and his wife went to visit. Tom is Charlotte's Godfather. That evening I joined Tom and Erica for the visit. I had about an hour with her and some of that time we spent alone together. I told Charlotte that she had suffered enough here on earth. I told her it was time for her suffering to end and ours to begin. I told her we'd all be okay and that I'd watch over Daddy for her. Her Daddy was the love of her life. Charlotte was Matt's world. He was the most amazing caretaker, father, nurse.... whatever she needed, Daddy had it covered. When we put her to bed, I kissed her head and told her I loved her with all my heart and that I was so thankful God chose her to be my granddaughter. I had hoped there would be more time but somehow, I knew this was it. Driving home that night, I cried all the way home and felt my heart breaking in two. I never knew pain this deep. I didn't know how we'd make it through once she was gone.

I didn't get there Tuesday night and hoped against all hope we'd have Wednesday evening for another visit. On Wednesday, June 22, 2022, a little after noon I got the call that Charlotte was gone. I remember screaming "NNNNOOOOOO"!!!! I heard what was said but I kept thinking "no, they must be wrong."

Charlotte's mom said she was breathing one minute and then she just stopped. I had to drive an hour from my office to get to her house to be with the family. I especially needed to be with my son. It was like being in a fog. When I arrived, I saw peace on her precious little face. She was finally done suffering. Her hand was still warm, so I held it for a bit. Charlotte fought long and hard, but it was finally her time. I have never felt such sadness. I was right there watching everything taking place and yet it felt surreal. I thought I'd wake up because this felt like a horrible nightmare. I held myself together for my son. It wasn't time for me to lose it, his baby girl just died. I needed to be strong for Matt. I got so good at being strong; in the days that followed, I couldn't cry. I just felt numb, broken, and empty. Seeing Matt's pain was what hurt the most in the days leading up to Charlotte's memorial service. His eyes were empty. The sadness dropped over him and totally enveloped him when Charlotte passed.

The death of a child is unimaginable. For a grandparent, we must endure our own pain, grief and broken heart and then there's your grown-up son or daughter who is completely destroyed by this. A mother can feel her children's pain more deeply than they them-selves do; their age doesn't matter. When Matt's heart broke, mine shattered. Nothing can help prepare you for any of this.

We survived Charlotte's memorial service—it was a celebration of her life. Memories were everywhere; so many pictures in photo albums, her cherished stuffed animals and a video was playing. Charlotte lived such a short time but filled every moment with bless-ings for all who knew her. So many people came to support us. Family, friends (both old and new), former co-workers and new co-workers... so many turned out to help us through this shocking devastation. We realized we are blessed to have such a strong support system. The service was beautiful. Aunt Vicki did a lovely eulogy, and the songs played were perfect. After the service, I received my cherished heart necklace with Charlotte's ashes. I wear it all the time. I can no longer hold my sweet girl, but I carry her with me every day. I think about the sweet little eyes looking up at me and listening so attentively and I can remember how happy we were together. Now I look at pictures of us together and I can see the love we shared from another point of view. Her beautiful little face leaning up towards mine with such soft beautiful eyes focused on my every word. Oh, how I loved her!

The time following Charlotte's passing is best described as the eye of a storm. It was beautiful, calm, peaceful and filled with people to hold us together. Flowers arrived, food baskets were delivered and so many cards filled our mailbox. I am blessed to work in an office filled with loving, compassionate people who surrounded me with friendship, love and prayers. Once life returned to "normal", the pain hit like a hurricane. I was lost in the undertow, being thrown to and fro with anguish. I wanted to help my son, but I didn't know how to when I couldn't even pull myself together. People made comments that I wasn't myself. I just suffered a horrible loss and didn't see any possible way to stop the pain in my chest. I remember just sitting and staring into space and realizing that I had just played through Charlotte's whole life in my head. I rode the rollercoaster through my head—good days, bad days, regular days, special days... they all mattered. Remembering the days with Charlotte was the only thing I wanted to do. All the days of Charlotte's life were the best days of my life. I just didn't understand how she left so suddenly. I wanted more time; we all needed more time, but she was gone. My brain understood but my heart just couldn't accept this. I felt empty, happiness was gone, joy was gone. I was left in a daze. Every day while driving home I would break down and cry. My commute is about fifty minutes. I would arrive home with red eyes and filled with sadness. Nothing could help me except being with Matt. When Matt and I were together, I was strong and held it together to help him.

Each day I would wake up in the morning, realize where I was, and then the pain came flooding back. Charlotte was gone. I always thought she'd pull through everything. How could pneumonia have taken her from us? It all happened so fast. I walked through the following days without any feeling, just broken. I was very lucky to work for a company that was supportive and understanding. I needed help, and I asked for it. Our company had coverage for emotional support if you need it. This was covered by our health insurance plan. I was connected to an amazing counselor named Catherine. She helped me to see it was ok to feel as I did. She explained this wouldn't last forever. What I learned is the depth of the loss comes from the depth of the love.

Charlotte was so loving, and our relationship was profound. We spoke to each other's hearts and minds without words. Whenever we were together, we took "selfies" and as soon as I held my phone up, Charlotte would pose. She would lean in, fold her arms and was ready for the picture. When she heard my voice in the house, she would make sweet little vocal sounds calling out to me to come see her. When I did, I was greeted by the most beautiful smiling face. I don't know how to go on in a world without Charlotte. The day Charlotte was born the sky was bright pink and the world was perfect. Now my whole world was grey and lonely.

Charlotte was unselfish. She was happy watching everyone around her having fun. She smiled seeing her brother and sister playing with friends. She loved watching her family going about the business of the day even though she couldn't join them. She never complained about her pain. She enjoyed the times that were hers. She loved bath time with her special chair, her tub toys and the music playlist Daddy had created for her. When she was a baby, she loved to watch her dancing bears go round and round above her in her swing. She would talk to them babbling as she told them stories. It was so precious to see. One of her favorite things was her room light that projected stars on her ceiling. She had this with her on multiple hospital trips. Someone donated a supply of these lights to CHOP so more children could experience the calming effect of these beautiful stars dancing on the ceiling. Charlotte's big sister Hailey was recently staying overnight at CHOP, and she received a light projector of her own and could now have the beautiful stars on her ceiling. This is Charlotte's legacy of love in a place that cared for her so often.

Charlotte had a way of bringing out the best in everyone. She was able to heal relationships that were broken for decades. That was her gift. She came to show love, acceptance, and peacefulness. She was one of God's rare children. Rare children are superheroes. They fight battles no one knows, but they are living examples of love and strength.

Grief is unavoidable when losing someone you love. It isn't a place to stay though. You will move through the stages and come to a place of acceptance. You can never forget. I won't forget the loss—I feel it every day. I read somewhere that eventually you grow and it's like scar tissue covers the saddest parts. I will miss Charlotte all the days of my life but I can cherish her and the love we shared until we meet again. I am comforted by the fact that I know she's in heaven waiting for me. She was pure, good, loving, and unchanged by this world. I can still feel her presence. No one knows what they can do because none of us have been in heaven to say for sure. It gives me great comfort to know she's well, healed and that we are still connected. Every now and then I feel a light touch on my arm or leg and I look around and I'm all alone. It's not my dog; it must be my sweet girl putting her hand on me to say hello. No one else is there. I know she's not far from me. We still communicate through our hearts and minds. I know she is whole now. She can walk, run, play, laugh, talk and is finally free from pain. That is what I wanted for her, freedom from pain. I am so thankful that I got to experience life with Charlotte. I would never trade a day of what we shared. The pain runs deep when the love does. A piece of my heart went home with Charlotte but a piece of Charlotte lives on in me. I will honor her memory by living life as she did. I will smile when someone greets me, try not to complain about pains I may have, enjoy the beauty in the world and live in the moment more often enjoying each day.

August 18, 2017 – June 22, 2022. The dash represents just four years and ten months of a beautiful life, a precious, well-loved little girl who changed lives. This chapter was written to honor the memory of the one, the only, the irreplaceable Charlotte Ruth Kessler. Until we meet again....

ABOUT THE AUTHOR

Marianne Young is a lifelong resident of Langhorne, PA. As an only child, Marianne was raised with an abundance of love and attention from her parents who instilled confidence in her abilities. Marianne has spent forty-two years in the Title Insurance industry as a Settlement Officer focusing on Customer Service.

Marianne has been married for seventeen years to her best friend and soul mate Ed. Together they have five grown children (and found one who feels like theirs), twelve grandchildren and an Akita named Fiona. Marianne loves spending time with her grandchildren, watching Netflix marathons, traveling and lying on the beach relaxing with a good book.

A life-long dream of Marianne's has been to write a book. Marianne dedicates this chapter to her precious granddaughter Charlotte who died on June 22, 2022, two months before her fifth birthday. Marianne shares her story to help others who have experienced a devastating loss.

> **Facebook:** *www.facebook.com/marianne.young.5*
> **Instagram:** *www.instagram.com/author_marianneyoung*
> **Linkedin:** *www.linkedin.com/in/mariannemyoung*

CHAPTER NINE

TURNING TRAUMA INTO TRIUMPH

MICHELLE MAGUIRE

As a young girl, I dreamed of the life I wanted when I grew up. I wanted to be married to a great man; have multiple children, a great career and a picture-perfect house, yes, the one with the white picket fence! I dreamed of all the things I would do with my family, all the places we would visit and the life that we would have. This vision carried on into my twenties, and at the age of twenty-five, I met a man who I thought to be "the one". We dated, talked for so many hours, and really enjoyed spending time together. We were so happy!

After six months, he proposed, and we were married a year and a half later. Life was great! I was doing well in my career, we took a few vacations, and had a great townhouse and then right before our first wedding anniversary, I found out I was pregnant! What more could anyone ask for, life was good, and the future that I wanted was unfolding right before my eyes. All my dreams that I had envisioned were coming true, and I couldn't be happier!

I loved being a mom right from the start. I loved the bond that was created and the family that we had started and even was adapting to a slightly different vision for my life. I was now a stay-at-home mom taking care of my son. I didn't want to miss any of his firsts or seconds for that matter. I had left my job toward the end of my pregnancy, and we were working toward saving money for a house so moving in with my parents was a blessing in so many ways. I was able to see the firsts and the seconds and so much more. I was able to watch him grow and although life was a little different, it was good until things started to take a turn.

Shortly after my son was fifteen months old, my husband and I, within a short time, had come into some health issues. It was a very scary time for us and a very challenging time as a newly married couple and new parents. We had so many unanswered questions and decisions to make. I remember being stunned, the feelings of uncertainty, fear and anger all at the same time. I was only thirty years old, a new mom, wife, and a lifetime ahead of me. This was not part of my dream or part of the plan, and I was so angry at God. I kept thinking it was a nightmare and I would wake up.

The year ahead was challenging, between work, surgeries, treatment, and trying to function normally all while navigating the situation and raising a young child. There was a lot of stress on us as a young couple but as bad as a year that it was, and not thinking there was going to be a light at the end of the tunnel, we survived and were stronger for it and looking back now, I am so grateful for how blessed we were on Christmas morning when I found out I was pregnant with my second son! It was truly a miracle as we were told by doctors that they didn't know if we would be able to have any more children. The faith that I lost when we got sick, was slowly returning—God was so good!

During this challenging time, I learned that life could really SUCK and that when it was so hard to see any light, you had to find faith, hope, and love. At that moment, I knew that life was going to turn around for us. In my heart I knew with faith, hope, love, and God by your side there was always a blessing that would come your way.

A few years went by and we began to struggle again but this time financially. The kids were in school, my husband and I were on different schedules, and we did fewer things together as a family and more just the boys and me. Money was tight as expenses started to rise. There was so much stress and a lot of arguing when we were together. It was very tense in the house, and you could see the happiness of our marriage and our family slipping away. The kids were becoming active, and my husband became depressed and began isolating himself as he just couldn't deal with anything. There were issues at work that then created problems at home. He found trouble easily and there were many times that you did not know what you would come home to. I tried to mask what was occurring from the kids, from family and friends. I figured if I kept us out of the house and if I painted the picture that everything was OK it would get better, but it didn't; it only got worse. I still tried to make our marriage work and tried to make our home as happy as I could. I didn't want to have a broken family. I didn't come from an environment like that and that is not what I wanted for my kids.

It took me several years to find the courage to leave as things would be better for a little while and then go south again. Yes, I would say it, but I couldn't do it. I had so many different emotions during this time as I didn't want to be the one who had a failed marriage. I didn't want my children to come from a broken home. I stayed, tried, and hid for several years and then I had enough. I deserved to be happy, my children deserved to be happy, and I had to figure it out and filed for divorce. Although the divorce started out amicable, over time that changed. There used to be communication and then that stopped. There was some involvement with the kids and then that stopped. It was always a constant battle, and I was always in emergency mode and dealing with constant chaos.

I never realized how divorce and the trauma that goes with it is like death. To heal you must grieve. You must go through the stages. I was stuck for a very long time as I blamed myself for a failed marriage and for not being able to fix a broken man and especially one that didn't care for anyone other than himself. I couldn't move past the trauma, because I hadn't allowed myself the time to process or the time to grieve. The pain had already hurt enough, I didn't want to feel what I needed to heal but I needed to find a way to do it.

It wasn't until fifteen months after losing my dad that I really stopped and thought about finding a way to heal and be happy again. I was so worried about always being there for my mom and my boys and my family that I neglected taking care of myself. I just did what I needed to do to get through the day, sometimes the hour. I really needed to take the time and do something for myself. I truly was just existing and not living for a long time. I was miserable, short-tempered and always on edge. It was not fair to anyone but especially not fair to my boys. I needed to find a way to feel whole and be happy to show my sons that life can really throw some wicked curveballs, but you can heal, grow, and overcome them. I want them to know that life is not always going to be that rough.

I had been following a friend on Facebook who had recently become a life coach and decided to try working with her and a group of women. It was the BEST decision I could have made and one that started to change my life. Kim helped me dig deep and deal with the trauma that I had encountered. She taught me how to accept grief and really go through the stages to be able to start to heal. She gave me a different perspective on what I had gone through and taught me that I needed to stop blaming myself for something that was out of my control. She allowed me to feel the emotions and discover my purpose.

A few months after I started working with Kim, I was ready to take things a step further and now work on the physical side of myself. I was already growing emotionally and spiritually, and I was starting to live again but throughout the process of healing I had turned to food to heal my emotions and it was time to stop that. I felt food was the answer and I needed to change that because didn't like what I looked like and was at an unhealthy weight. Walking up the stairs had become a challenge. I was always tired and I just didn't feel right. I decided to take another chance and begin a program that helped you change your habits, which leads to changing your mindset. Again, the BEST decision I made for myself. This program helped me continue to look deeper into who I am and who I want to be, it helped me to stay focused and to discover why I did certain behaviors and how I could start to retrain my mind. I was growing, my mindset was changing, and I was discovering who I am. I was gaining the confidence that I had lost. I was losing weight and I was changing my life one habit and one day at a time. I was happy! I am happy! I can look myself in the mirror again and like what I see. I am proud of who I am, and life is good again!

Going through the process of healing has allowed me to discover who I am. I had so many people help me during the challenging times and always being there for me that now it is the time for me to give back. I was determined to show my sons that no matter how difficult life gets, it does not define you. I wanted to find a way to help others and for others to know that they are not alone, so I took another leap and became an independent life and health coach. I now help others meet their life and health goals and discover their why. I walk the journey with them.

Life is not easy and there will always be bumps in the road, but these are the lessons that we need to learn in life. The trauma, the grief and everything in between helps us to grow and to live the life that we are meant to live.

ABOUT THE AUTHOR

Michelle Maguire is a single mother of two teenage sons and manages a full-time career. She has worked in the healthcare industry for over twenty years and recently has become an independent life and health coach. Michelle enjoys being her boy's greatest fan and cheerleader and loves spending time at the beach, her happy place. Throughout life, she has experienced multiple life-changing events, yet remained devoted to raising her children and helping others. This is Michelle's first time sharing her story of trauma and grief. Focus, faith and hope provided the strength to successfully navigate through these challenging times. It is Michelle's hope that sharing her experiences will provide inspiration and motivation to others. You are not alone, and Michelle's tenacity proves you can manage and persevere through the challenges life presents. She is excited to pay it forward and is thankful for the life lessons she has learned throughout her journey.

Facebook Group: www.fb.me/michellemaguirecoaching
Instagram: www.instagram.com/michellemaguire-coaching

CHAPTER TEN

SILENT SUFFERING

SHANNON PASSALACQUA

T his wasn't supposed to be my calling. This isn't how I had envisioned my life or where I thought the road would take me. And yet, I kept getting pulled back to this thought, to this nagging, intrusive thought that kept begging the question "but what if this is what all the pain was for?"

My husband, Joe, and I had experienced six miscarriages—yes, you read that right, six. This is the point when I like to make people feel better about our losses by letting them know that we have three living children, a daughter from his previous marriage and two boys. I feel the need to tell this to people as if it somehow takes away from the pain we experienced with our six losses. "At least you're able to have children." One of those qualifiers to make the trauma less significant. To make others feel ok with our pain.

If I'm to be honest, when I was going through my miscarriages, I believed those qualifiers, those statements. "Give it time" or "Don't worry, just try again" or "Be grateful for what you have". Each time I would hear those statements, they would pierce my heart, but I would tell myself that they must be true, that I just need to move on and get over it. I had never experienced grief in my life and didn't know what to do with it, so I just ignored it. I swept it under the rug and assumed it would just go away, especially if I got pregnant again and was able to hold a baby in my arms.

I was so wrong.

Before I open my heart to you, I want to be clear about a couple of things. My miscarriages changed my life. For the good. They eviscerated me from the inside out, throwing everything that I thought I knew out the window so that I had to completely start over and question my past stories. It is impossible to explain with ink and paper just how traumatic and how much pain those losses were for us. But sometimes what we create from the broken pieces is much more beautiful than the perfect, uncracked version we were before.

Our life was pretty perfect. I don't say that as a cliché or to make anyone feel bad, it just was. We had experienced typical stress: paying the bills, work, normal marriage arguments, etc. We were coasting through our lives. Until we started trying for a second baby. Our first pregnancy had been so easy, a very typical pregnancy with no complications. So, when we started to try again, we assumed that it would be just as easy. We celebrated the positive pregnancy test. The pregnancy symptoms always started early for me and therefore I always knew when I was pregnant earlier than most other women. I looked forward to reaching the twelve-week mark when my symptoms would dissipate, and I would start feeling normal again. So, when I woke up a few days after the positive pregnancy test feeling nothing I was pretty happy! I was relieved that this time I wouldn't be feeling the nausea as much. I'm not sure how long after I woke up, probably in the shower, when I noticed that all my symptoms were gone including my breast tenderness that I started to become anxious. I grabbed my phone and started researching what this could mean. This was of no help. It seemed that there was no information out there about disappearing pregnancy symptoms.

So, I took another test. The line was still there. I was relieved. But why was the line fainter? Did that mean anything? Again, I picked up my phone. Again, it was of no help. Everything said that if there is a line, no matter how faint, you are pregnant. I convinced myself I was ok and went on with my day. And then I started bleeding. I took another test. The line was even lighter. I started questioning myself. Had I been pregnant? Had there been a line before? I felt like I was crazy. I had no idea what was happening, so I called my doctor and explained everything to the receptionist. Her tone in her response told me everything "It sounds like you are having a chemical pregnancy. I'm really sorry". I hung up the phone in shock. I didn't know what to feel. I didn't even understand what was happening or what was going to happen. I spent hours researching "chemical pregnancy" and with every answer, I ended up with two more questions. What is a chemical pregnancy? Had I actually been pregnant? Why does it happen? What is going to happen? Can I try again? When? Did I cause this?

With these questions enveloping me, never once did I ask how to heal. Never once did I think of looking for support to help me with my grief. What I did instead was crawl under my covers and cry alone, truly believing that I could just wait it out and I would go back to "normal" soon.

Normal never returned.

The next month we experienced our second miscarriage. Two months later we experienced our third. By this point, I had fallen into what you might label as a routine or a ritual. I would receive a positive pregnancy test. It was supposed to be a gift, but those tests started feeling like ticking time bombs. I became obsessive with the testing. I was buying so many tests that I started going to different pharmacies throughout town because I was afraid that the cashiers would start recognizing me. I would line them up to compare them, analyzing just how dark the second line was. Was it getting lighter? Staying the same? I started hiding them from my husband, afraid that he would question just how crazy I had become. When I would start to bleed or when the test line became fainter, I would grab my glass of wine, Advil and tissue, lock myself in my room and cry.

Our lives became consumed by pregnancy tests, ovulation tests, blood work, doctor appointments and more losses. I noticed all the labels used, chemical pregnancy, recurrent pregnancy loss (RPL), spontaneous abortion, and HCG levels and I started using them to label myself. I was the girl who had the miscarriages. I was the girl who couldn't do what she was "supposed" to do. I completely lost myself. I lost my connection to who I was to myself, who I was to my husband and who I was to the world. I was drowning in the grief and the trauma.

One day, on my way to work, I stopped by the doctor's office to have yet another blood draw. We had received a positive pregnancy test a couple days prior, but I had started to have cramping the previous night and was asked to come in to have some blood drawn. At this point, my body had experienced four miscarriages and I knew what that pain meant. There are some events in your life that are stamped in your memory in slow motion, and this was one of them for me. I was standing outside my classroom when my doctor called to give me the results of the blood draw. "Your HCG levels have more than doubled. You are definitely still pregnant". I burst into tears and almost collapsed to the ground. I couldn't believe what I was hearing; I hadn't lost this one.

I never let myself get excited. I kept telling myself when I get to twelve weeks I'll relax. When I get to twenty weeks, I'll be happy. When I get past twenty-five weeks, when the baby would be viable if born, I would feel joy. I never felt those emotions. We lived in constant fear for nine months. We wouldn't buy anything for the baby for fear that it would jinx the pregnancy. I told myself that once I was holding my baby, I would let go of those fears and that everything would go back to normal, and I would be back to myself again. Our baby boy was born, healthy and happy. But I never returned to myself.

Grief changes you. I'm not quite sure why this is such a secret, everyone will experience grief at some point in their lives, but it does change you. You can learn to hold hands with grief, and you can learn to experience joy and connection again, but grief is always with you. The pain doesn't go away, you just learn to grow with it. And you can either learn to embrace it while living a vibrant life, or you can continue to let it consume you. I let it consume me. It wasn't until our fifth loss that it dawned on me that I couldn't continue to live the way I was living, just going through the motions, not fully living.

I was already six weeks pregnant when I found out. I had just stopped nursing and didn't notice the changes in my body or my period. This pregnancy came as a surprise and we, hesitantly, welcomed it. I was past the point where I normally had miscarriages, so we foolishly believed that were out of the woods. Due to my history, my doctor wanted to keep a close eye on this pregnancy. At our eight-week appointment, the doctor noticed that the baby hadn't grown as much as was expected. He wanted to check me again in a week. The waiting is the hardest part. You're living your life in limbo, not knowing if you will be a family of four or if you will be torn apart again. The following appointment showed that everything was back on track and the baby was indeed, still growing. Until it wasn't. A couple weeks later I started to spot. I called my doctor from work, and they asked me to come in when the school day was over. I told them it was probably just implantation bleeding, that I was past the time I normally had my miscarriages. They still wanted to see me.

"There's no heartbeat". I'm fairly certain those are the worst words a person can ever hear. With just one sentence, three little words strung together, you've become a coffin. All the hopes and dreams, all the little flutters and changes in your body have literally died inside of you. Miscarriage is a unique death. It's the only type of death that happens inside a person. You aren't just mourning the loss of your baby, but you are actually witnessing it happen inside your body, the body that was supposed to protect it and give it life. I opted to have a D&C. I knew that I couldn't bear the physical and emotional pain of delivering a miscarriage on my own. I woke up from the D&C feeling empty. I felt like an organ was missing, like I was hollow inside. But it wasn't a missing organ, it was a missing baby.

That was the loss that changed me. That was the loss that made me stop everything I was doing and ask myself "why?" Why was God or the Universe putting me through so much pain? What was I supposed to do with all of this pain? I wasn't sure what the answer was but I knew I was going to use this to help other women. A few months after our fifth loss, we experienced another early loss and that solidified my future.

How does a person go from feeling like a coffin to being able to help others? How do you move on from being a label, from being an HCG level, from being a statistic (one in four pregnancies end in miscarriage and one in hundred women will experience RPL)? A lot of very large steps as well as little decisions. First you need to recognize that trauma has occurred and that healing needs to take place. For me, this came in a lot of different forms. I knew I wasn't my old self and that I was disconnected. But I didn't know how to change it or why I even felt this way. I was telling my friend, who happens to be a therapist, about my miscarriages. There were certain details that I couldn't remember and when I commented on how weird it was that I couldn't remember details of events that had completely changed the fabric of who I was, she responded with "It's not weird at all. It's called a trauma response."

Trauma.

Trauma is exactly what I had been through but hadn't had the language to describe. I had spent over a year of my life living in a state of fear, living in a state of fight or flight. I had rewired my brain to live in anxiety and fear and to delay any joyful emotions. I had essentially taught myself to not be happy and that any time I felt connected to anything, it would be ripped from me and therefore it wasn't safe for me to feel a connection. And that's where I began my healing journey.

I spent the next years reading anything I could get my hands on about grief, trauma and healing. I soaked in these books, podcasts and research articles and used all of the knowledge to work on myself. I started feeling sparks inside of me, like I was coming back to life. In the healing after my babies' deaths, I was reborn.

There's a picture of me and my family on Halloween. In this picture, as you might suspect, we are all dressed up in our costumes, ready for the big night. If you looked at this picture you would see a happy family. When I look at this picture, I see my suffering. I was still recovering from our D&C, still bleeding and in pain. That night we went to a friend's house. Everyone there knew what we had just been through and yet, no one asked about it. No one asked how I was doing or simply said "I'm so sorry you are going through this". I was expected to paint a smile on my face and be strong for everyone else when all I wanted was for one person to talk about my baby.

We need support. We need to feel like people care. We need to be able to talk about our loss and tell our stories. We need community. Community is a necessary part of healing. Grief needs to be witnessed. You need to know that your story, your baby, your dream mattered. The medical community and our society can make you feel like your losses don't matter, like the death of your baby and your dreams didn't actually count. But they do.

For some of us, community is enough to help us heal. For a lot of us, it isn't, and we need to learn HOW to grieve and the tools to help us process that grief and trauma. In 2020 a research paper was released by the Journal of Gynecology and Obstetrics that twenty percent of women will experience PTSD, anxiety or depression after a miscarriage. And yet, there is a huge lack of resources for women to learn how to cope with this loss. When we are in the doctor's office, we need to be held, supported and heard. We need to know that yes, this happens to a lot of women, but that doesn't mean it doesn't hurt. Women need our society to acknowledge our pain, to witness it and to be able to sit with it. We need to learn how to find joy again and rewire our brains to notice and experience joy and happiness. We need to learn how to give ourselves permission to collapse in grief but also permission to rise back after that collapse. This is why I created the free Miscarriage Warrior App, a safe, loving community where you feel safe to grieve your loss while learning tools to help you heal.

As a woman experiencing one of the most traumatic experiences in her life, she needs to be given a space to feel her loss as well as tools to help her heal. Instead of just pushing it aside and hoping that it doesn't happen again, a woman needs to learn how to notice the feelings, how to name them and acknowledge them as well as how to move them through her body and out of her body. Healing is not just a one-time event. It doesn't just happen and then everything is fine on the other side. Healing takes time and is a journey. Sometimes healing can be painful and sometimes healing can be beautiful. But healing is well worth all of the emotions and to be able to find your connection to yourself again, to be able to live a life knowing that you have lost so much while also knowing that you hurt because you loved.

My miscarriages changed me. They made me stronger, but they also made me softer. They made me stop and realize that everyone has been through loss and deserves love and compassion. My miscarriages also showed me how much more work our society needs to learn about supporting a woman experiencing such loss. They showed me just how much we need community and a place to feel seen and loved. They showed me how important it is to feel all of our feelings, not just the good ones. And most importantly, they showed me that you can be broken, lying in a puddle on the bathroom floor but that you will be ok and you will put yourself together again. You may not look the same and it may be a difficult process, but you will be ok and you are not alone.

ABOUT THE AUTHOR

Shannon Passalacqua found her calling after experiencing six miscarriages and recognizing that there wasn't a safe space for women to grieve this unique loss. Shannon created the Miscarriage Warrior App to provide a community for women to grieve as well as learn tools to guide their healing journey. Through her own grief and healing journey, she learned that there is a cost when we avoid our grief and she wanted to ensure that no other women experience this grief alone as well as bring this topic more attention so that women receive the support they need. Shannon uses her degrees in psychology and education and her certificate as a High-Performance Coach to help women feel safe to grieve and find their connection to themselves and vibrancy in their lives again. To explore the different services Shannon provides, please visit her website.

> ***App store:*** *www.apps.apple.com/us/app/miscarriage-warrior/id1533455989*
> ***Website:*** *www.elevatedcoaching.coach*
> ***Instagram:*** *www.instagram.com/miscarriage_warrior*

CHAPTER ELEVEN

I'M STRONGER THAN MY GRIEF

ZAKIYYAH M. AUSTIN

A long time ago, I realized that I don't accept death well and know that I'm not the only one who struggles with letting go. I'm pretty sure I make people feel uncomfortable by how long I am stricken with grief; however, that would be their business. Every person copes with their own experiences in their own way so I don't expect anyone to feel how I feel about anything on any subject. I had three women who shaped my life as a human, woman, and mother.

I said "had" because I lost all three and today, I still talk to them aloud in the areas that they each molded me. I remember witnessing my grandmother work 2nd shift after getting up early to enjoy her cup of instant coffee, read the newspaper, and do some house chores before getting off to work. At every opportunity, I would sit with her, and she would share her coffee with me (probably why I love a good cup of coffee today). My grandmother loved caramel squares and as I write these words it's bringing a smile to my face because I prefer caramel-flavored coffee—thanks, Nanah. These three women were my rocks and they were each other's rocks.

FUCK CANCER! In 1998, my grandmother fought a good fight

with colon cancer and it pained me deeply to see her breaking down. I recall stopping by to see her one night to find her on her knees crying in pain. I was helpless! What could I do to help my Nanah feel better? Nothing! The matriarch was suffering and so was I because I looked up to her as my super woman; she was perfect. Nanah was a tough one and this disease was weakening her. I would stop by more often, when I left, I would just sit in my car sobbing because I was helpless and our time was quickly running out. When she went to be with the lord that was my very first bout of depression; I felt anger.

I then witnessed my aunt and mother cope with grief, and they leaned on one another to get through the familiar pain they were feeling. Those two ladies were inseparable, which later proved that heartbreak can kill you.

In 2004, my aunt fought her good fight with breast cancer. She was my Retsy! I was closer with my aunt than my mother during my teen years because I was a product of my urban environment (hello, Essex County). I stayed in trouble breaking curfews, fighting often, and everything else a rebellious girl could "attempt" to get away with. I found myself in a few precincts due to fighting, and I knew better than to call my mother first. My aunt had my back and when she spoke up for me, my mother knew she was not to be challenged. Her words to me in 2004 (I was becoming a mom) that I can still vividly hear her say... "God won't put anything on you that you cannot handle". I later had to lean on those words again in my very own battle. At this time, she was recently diagnosed with cancer and I was nervous! Not you too, not my savior, I was determined to be present and supportive for her. I remember trying to get her to incorporate more of a holistic diet. I have never been a fan of commercial medicine and I did not have faith that any of it would extend her days. She was willing to try, at first, she went into remission and we thought we won. The ladies went on a cruise, and when she came back her voice was different; I was nervous all over again because it lingered and lingered. Here we go, the cancer has reared its ugly head again! How can you prepare yourself to lose someone who means so much to you? Someone who I revered for her strength is being broken down day after day right before our eyes. I knew she was afraid, she was different, less Retsy (feisty). I was fortunate enough that she witnessed me mature from the wild child she protected and rescued on several occasions to the poised mother I became. When my aunt went to be with their mom in heaven, my mom was deeply stricken with grief and loneliness. I was hoping I could feel her void with my daughters. I knew she was not ok and those closest to her knew she was not ok. I think everyone who loved her deeply tried to keep her busy and distracted. Now, this is where I probably first noticed that every smile doesn't mean happiness or normalcy. Some smiles and laughter are surface. I later learned how to perfect this façade.

In 2008, at age fifty my beloved mother went to bed to not open her eyes, ever again. The morning I got that call was like a piercing through my heart! I probably replayed those gut-wrenching words way too many times "mommy isn't waking up!" My sister heard the alarm go off; however, mommy didn't quiet it as usual. I cannot imagine what she felt when she walked into the room to discover a lifeless mother lying in bed in the next room over. My grief is not the same as her grief, even today. So many people thought it was comforting to say "at least she didn't suffer". Those words landed on deaf ears at that time. I had plans for us! I needed her! I had two small daughters who loved their grandmother dearly. Mom's primary care physician didn't understand what caused her untimely death because her recent visit and stress test did not show any signs to be concerned about. In my opinion, GRIEF overwhelmed her. I could not get myself together for months, ok years! I was introduced to Reiki and psychotherapy as my coping mechanisms. I was constantly questioning God. I wanted answers! Good Grief, I felt like I lost my mother and my father! Who was I going to lean on now? I felt abandoned. When I lost my mom, I took months out of work to gather myself. I signed up for weekly therapy sessions that lasted somewhere around nine months. I needed someone to help me understand my feelings. I was wondering if I missed any signs. My ladies were all together again and I was heartbroken at a depth I was not familiar with. I talk to them when I need advice. I let them know that I miss them, but I am not ready to be with them. I believe it's important to be precise because my mom possibly told Nanah and Retsy that she missed them so they came to reunite with her. I've had encounters where I feel like they intervened to keep me alive. Do you believe in angels? I do! Months after her passing, I was often visited by her spirit and it scared me. I knew it was her; at least I wanted to feel her presence so much that I claimed it as her. I have kept her memorial card in every vehicle I've owned since 2008 because I know my angel has me covered in her wings.

I finally picked myself up, finally focused on my reasons to live, then...WHAM! My angels saved MY life! They knew I wasn't ready; they weren't ready to have me either. Death is promised to each of us, yes that's certain, but why does it have to cut so deep?

My celebration of life resulted in the loss of life and a twelve-day fight to survive. This experience had me drowning in feelings and pain I never could have imagined. We hear of others going through traumatic events and naturally we feel empathy. However, it does not last long if it's not direct to our lives. On September 07, 2019, I along with three friends and a half-sister took a weekend trip to Atlanta, GA, to celebrate my 43rd birthday. Within 24-hours only four of us were alive, two barely. We were in a fiery auto collision. By the grace of God, I pulled through after twelve days. When I did pull through enough to have a conscious conversation, I vaguely recall trying to grasp my surroundings. I was quizzed on where I was and informed on how I got there. I had multiple scars and wounds that instantly became emotionally ingrained and several physically permanent. I asked how each person was doing and I heard about the status of three; however, one was avoided. After a few times throughout that day of asking about "Sunshine" it became painfully obvious that something unthinkable was the outcome. Everyone I asked would walk out of the room or try to change the subject. I was in shock when my sister, Hayat, finally came out and admitted what I believed to be the answer...Sunshine did not survive. I was in shock to the extent that I just laid there. No sound, just numb! Is this real?! Am I truly here? Did we actually encounter this? I didn't and still don't remember some events of that day or evening. I was desperately trying to process what the fuck I just heard and my physical condition. I had multiple fractures, burns, and my face was severely scarred, and I could barely move. Wait...it's one of us who hasn't regained consciousness, my TiTah! Oh God, please have mercy on my best friend. Sunshine had already been buried and all I could think of was her three children and grandchildren. She was so present in their lives and all I wanted was to speak to them, I didn't know what I wanted to say besides, "SORRY!" I AM SO SORRY that your mom didn't return home in the same manner that she left NJ. No words were comforting to me, so I knew it wasn't much I could say to them, but I needed and still want to express my deepest condolences.

Let another round of grief flourish, one where I felt guilt for surviving. I tried to remember our last day...I wanted to remember our last conversations, the jokes we laughed at. Sunshine was full of jokes! Everyone was in such great spirits all day. TiTah said we were having a "hot girl summer" at least for the weekend. We had plans to party and bullshit all weekend long and rest on our return home. TiTah was grieving a recent loss, Sunshine was celebrating a huge win, and I was in need of an escape from a turbulent relationship. We just wanted to have a good weekend without thinking about our realities back home. Twenty-seven days in Grady Memorial Hospital, Atlanta, Georgia and sixty-two days in JFK Hospital back home in Edison, New Jersey. I cannot explain how miserable I was. My childhood best friend was still unconscious in Georgia; I was kept updated on her status through her partner and other friends who continued to look after her. I was trying my hardest to see how/if she could be transferred to JFK Hospital because they are known for successfully treating brain injuries. No such luck; three months after the remaining of us were discharged, TiTah succumbed to her injuries. My physical condition did not allow me to make it to see her and the pandemic being at its highest devastation reduced her bedside support. My sister showed up at my house that morning, March 25, 2020, at 4:30 a.m. and she didn't have to say anything. It was the look on her face; I lost my shit! NOOOO was all I could muster through the overflow of tears. Lord, help me! Give me strength I don't know I have! My days became very dark, my heart was shattered, and I was questioning why I survived. Again, WHY did this happen, what happened out there, how did I get so lucky to be alive? For too many hours I was alone with my thoughts and believe me, they were eating me up! I strapped myself into an emotional rollercoaster. There were days and nights that I cried silently and aloud. I felt guilty for smiling, laughing, and having any bit of fun. This guilt lasted more than two years; each day is different. Today, I am holding on to faith because the etched memory of it all weighs me down. Today, not every day is a good day for me, physically or mentally. My birthdays are not as "happy". I'd rather stay in bed, no phone, no company, no noise! My birthday is now a double sword of life and death. Three years later, I finally enjoyed a day celebrating with those who showed up for me during my recovery period, relentlessly and those who reminded me of more pleasant times. The times when life was full of kicks and giggles; no grief at all. The times when everyone dear to me was still alive and available for me to spend quality time with.

You may wonder how I managed? Daily prayer, frequent reiki, self-help and motivational books, crystals, psychotherapy, and the support of family and friends got me to this point of sanity. The year 2020 was very dark for me. I was still having surgeries, lots of painful physical therapy, fought off a bad case of COVID-19, and survivor's remorse was suffocating me. I was fake smiling and pretending to be fine. Understand that I am grateful to be alive today, I've regained a majority of my independence, and I'm still here for my two daughters; thank you, God. I grieve for my friends' families, I grieve for my physical condition now having limitations, I grieve for my romantic relationship that has suffered, I grieve for the loss of the invaluable relationships of two women I can honestly say were "friends". I grieve for the activities and career I can no longer enjoy. I'm stronger today spiritually and physically, thanks to my God. I speak for the other two survivors when I say that it hasn't been an easy trek. It was not easy to accept the challenges that came with the injuries and survival; however, I am resilient! I have daughters and other family members who rely on my strength and it was much more important to me to make sure I fought to regain as much of myself as I could. I've changed because of prayer and gratitude for my existence. I see the world through a different lens today. I've met other survivors recently and it is unanimous that we value each day more than we did prior to our life-threatening events. Speaking for myself, I have no mental capacity or tolerance for negativity, I do not wish to spend time with or on anything that challenges my peace. Survival did that for me. Grief can go unrecognized because many times it is concealed with an empty smile. Some days are so heavy that people just give up. I was never suicidal because I felt like I fought too hard to pull through those life-threatening injuries in 2019, I can't possibly wimp out now. I grew up as a fighter and I still have fight in me when it's required. I want to send love and support to anyone who feels over-whelmed by grief. Whatever it is that you are grieving, find some-thing worth standing up for. I was told twice during my darkest days that it could have been worse for me. Of course, I knew that and guess what? I needed to hear it at that moment. When I feel down on myself about how I walk different today, I think about those who can't walk. When I allow negative thoughts about my current phys-ical condition to creep in, I lean on gratitude. I am extremely grateful to have healed to the extreme that I have healed. I invested in my healing mentally, emotionally, and financially. If I did not push myself, what else should I have expected to receive? Minimal recovery and drugs for depression. I mentioned previously, I'm not one for the prescriptions and commercial drugs. I do believe that if your burdens, pains, and diagnosis call for prescriptions then, you must do what it takes to survive! Survival feels good today, however, this was a full journey that had a few setbacks that allow me to embrace this feeling. I go to bed in gratitude and I wake up in gratitude because it took twelve days for me to open my eyes with sight, my brain with independent function, my original body parts intact (including hardware), and the sarcasm that I would have been sad to lose. (I have jokes too!) Life can be short, it's definitely full of surprises, so don't think too much about what you should do; just figure out how to get it done. Grief, depression, anxiety, and loneliness can rob you of so many opportunities and positive experiences. Advice: acknowledge what you are feeling, ask for help, pray regularly and be precise about your asking. Protect and embrace your superpower! Give yourself life in a way that may be uncomfortable to the familiar you; be bold and brave for the version of you that is rising. The world is now full of resources that are accessible from the comfort of your home and in my previous situation (the hospital bed) where the only excuse is the one you accept for yourself. YouTube helped me sleep on many restless nights. It helped me strengthen my faith, it helped me advance my career, and it continues to help many of us in various ways, free of charge. Tap in! I want to hear about your survival of grief or simply your survival and gratitude for life on my channels.

ABOUT THE AUTHOR

Zakiyyah Austin was born and raised in Essex County, New Jersey. She is a mom to two daughters and is an entrepreneur and a survivor. Zakiyyah has an insurance agency, the Z Austin Agency in Woodbridge, NJ, where she also raised her daughters and enjoyed a real estate career for more than ten years. She holds a securities license and is extremely passionate about helping others by sharing invaluable information, connecting people, and through her insurance work. Zakiyyah, believes authentic partnerships are priceless and very necessary in various aspects of life. After a near-death experience, Zakiyyah lives life with pure gratitude for each day. She believes you learn so much about yourself and the people around you when you take time to simply still yourself, your mind, and press reset on your energy to re-focus. In her words, "Manage your thoughts and be kind to others...the rewards are bountiful."

Website: www.whatisurvived.com
Shop my Etsy store: www.etsy.com/shop/whatisurvived
Get life insurance by visiting: www.zaustinagency.com
Learn about energy and frequency healing: www.
　　healenergetically.com
Facebook: www.facebook.com/profile.php?id=
　　100086055145931

REFLECTION

We've intentionally left the following pages open for you.
Feel free to write your reflections from the stories you've read, share
your own story, or jot down anything your heart feels drawn to
explore.

REFLECTION

REFLECTION

REFLECTION

REFLECTION

REFLECTION

REFLECTION

REFLECTION

REFLECTION

ABOUT THE PUBLISHER
& MELISSA CHERNOW

Ironically, Melissa never took to reading growing up. The fictional novels assigned in school left her heart desiring more: she always sought real stories from real people. The human experience was her muse, and she wanted to learn about it from as many people as were willing to share theirs.

Her healing journey has consisted of two main themes: learning to trust her intuition, and reclaiming her voice. The former led to the latter, and it also led to multi-author books. She fell in love with this style of publishing because it offers real stories, multiple perspectives, a healing experience for authors and readers alike, honors creative expression, and builds community.

Melissa founded Cardinal Publishing House to honor the depth and breadth of our lived experiences. We are an indie publisher devoted to building community through storytelling. We focus on the somatic journey of storytelling, letting your body and intuition lead the way to share the story that wants to move through you. Cardinal Publishing House would love to support your storytelling and leadership journey.

Melissa Chernow
Founder, Cardinal Publishing House
Somatic Voice & Visibility Coach

FURTHER ASSISTANCE

If you or someone you know is struggling, please know you are not alone and reach out for help.

Suicide Prevention Hotline
United States: Dial 988

Talk Suicide Canada
Canada: 1-833-456-4566

Lifeline
Australia: 13 11 14

Better Help
www.betterhelp.com